Ace and Aro Journeys

of related interest

How to Be Ace
A Memoir of Growing Up Asexual
Rebecca Burgess
ISBN 978 1 78775 215 3
eISBN 978 1 78775 216 0

How to Understand Your Sexuality
A Practical Guide for Exploring Who You Are
Meg-John Barker and Alex Iantaffi
Illustrated by Jules Scheele
ISBN 978 1 78775 618 2
eISBN 978 1 78775 619 9

Ace Voices
What it Means to Be Asexual, Aromantic, Demi or Grey-Ace
Eris Young
ISBN 978 1 78775 698 4
eISBN 978 1 78775 699 1

Sounds Fake But Okay
An Asexual and Aromantic Perspective on Love,
Relationships, Sex, and Pretty Much Anything Else
Sarah Costello and Kayla Kaszyca
ISBN 978 1 83997 001 6
eISBN 978 1 83997 002 3

ACE and ARO JOURNEYS

A Guide to Embracing Your Asexual or Aromantic Identity

❖ ❖ ❖ ❖

The Ace and Aro Advocacy Project

Jessica Kingsley Publishers
London and Philadelphia

First published in Great Britain in 2023 by Jessica Kingsley Publishers
An imprint of Hodder & Stoughton Ltd
An Hachette UK Company

I

Copyright © The Ace and Aro Advocacy Project 2023

A CIP catalogue record for this title is available from the
British Library and the Library of Congress

ISBN 978 1 83997 638 4
eISBN 978 1 83997 639 1

Printed and bound in the United States by Integrated Books International

Jessica Kingsley Publishers' policy is to use papers that are natural,
renewable and recyclable products and made from wood grown in sus-
tainable forests. The logging and manufacturing processes are expected to
conform to the environmental regulations of the country of origin.

Jessica Kingsley Publishers
Carmelite House
50 Victoria Embankment
London EC4Y 0DZ

www.jkp.com

To all aro and ace people, whether you know it yet or not—we hope this book helps show you the world of possibilities open to you and helps guide you towards the life you want to live.

List of authors

Nathan Bernstein
Kadie Craighead
Sirena Davidson
Quargs Greene
Maximus Jenkins
Emily Karp
Cecil Lune
Lari McBunker

And several other authors who chose to remain unlisted.

Artists

Cecil Lune
Dee Harris
Mido Vince
Nicola Powling

Contents

Contents

Acknowledgments

From TAAAP: Thank you to all the other advocates involved in TAAAP who didn't write this book but provided moral support, answers to confused questions, feedback, and more. Thanks also to TAAAP advocates Dave, who contributed tremendously to the writing, and Hannah for help with revising and editing!

Thanks to JKP Publishing and our editor, Andrew James, for helping us get this book from the more formal and academic version to where it is now. Thanks to Nicola Powling for the cover design and to Mido Vince, Cecil Lune, and Dee Harris for creating the foundational concept that it was based on!

Thanks to scholars and researchers Nicolette K Robbins, Kathryn Graff Low, and Anna N Query for publishing the research on an asexual identity model that inspired the premise of this book. We are also indebted to all of the aromantic and asexual activists, writers, researchers, and journalists whose work makes this world a better place for all of us.

Most of all, thank you to all of the aro and ace people who trusted us enough to give us your stories—the responses to our questionnaires not only gave us every quote throughout the book's pages, but also informed each step of writing this book. Without you, this book could not exist.

From Nathan: A special shout-out to my dad, Dan Nathan, both because he would answer questions about what attraction feels like, and because he made me promise that I would mention and thank him. To my mom, Dori Bernstein, for being my ethical role model in pretty much every circumstance and always encouraging and believing in me. Thanks to both of them for supporting me every step of the way both in my own aroace journey and in writing this book. I can't even express how lucky I am to have people who accept me for who I am and let me figure out who I want to be with no expectations.

Thanks also to Judy Bernstein talking me through an allo therapist's perspective and to Louisa Nathan for being the best big sister ever and getting me lots of excellent socks. And to Rita, for attending and distracting me during many a book meeting.

From Kadie: Thank you to my therapist, Katie, for trusting in me, standing by me, and helping me to be the person I am today. Thank you Aly and Aubrey for being so supportive and totally open-minded. You are so beautiful. I love you. Finally, thank you to all the brilliant people in TAAAP who made writing this book fun, explorative, and one-of-a-kind. You are my friends and inspiration. It's been an honor.

From Sirena: Thanks to my friend for being with me through all the challenges and joys of helping to write this book. Thanks as well to everyone in TAAAP for helping these communities and giving me a place to help too.

From Emily: I greatly appreciate how fortunate I am to have so many friends, family members, partners I've dated, and even therapists who have been supportive of me this past decade as I embraced my own ace and aro identities and figured out the nuances of what my own boundaries and desires are. I additionally feel privileged to have been able to forge many friendships with ace and aro individuals – through the online ace blogosphere, fandom communities, my local Washington, DC based meetup group, as well as TAAAP itself. Thank you so much to all of you - each of you play a key role in my own ace and aro journey.

Introduction

Who Are We?

The Ace and Aro Advocacy Project (TAAAP) is a group that works to advocate for inclusion, respect, and understanding of all the different ways that someone may relate to or engage in romantic or sexual attraction and relationships, with a focus on the asexual (ace) and aromantic (aro) communities while understanding that everyone, whether ace, aro, or neither, deserves these same considerations. Aro and ace people can define their orientations in an assortment of ways, use varying identity labels within the ace and aro spectrums, have differing levels of privilege due to their other identities, have diverse backgrounds related to romantic and sexual activity, and have different life experiences that cause each individual to have a unique relationship to their orientation.

Our team reflects some of the diversity present in the communities—we are a variety of orientations, races, genders, religions, ages, disabilities, and neurodivergencies, etc. In writing this book, we strive to include many of these perspectives and experiences that are beyond our own.

So What Is This Book?

This book is a discussion of the process of understanding and embracing identity. As people who have lived with ace and aro identities for varying periods of time, we believe that there is a lack of resources that specifically address the influences on how people discover, relate to, and interact with aromantic and asexual identities. There is plenty of informal content out there about these topics, including personal blogs and art, but as valuable as these perspectives are, they are not easy to find unless you are already in the community and aware of asexuality and aromanticism. For those who do not know what aromanticism and asexuality are, do not have access to online or in-person communities, or only know of these orientations through someone who identifies as such, it can be difficult to gain deep and informative knowledge about how people live with these orientations. In writing this book, we hope to reach these often-underserved ace and aro people, as well as to provide a comprehensive path to understanding for all aro and ace people. We also hope this book aids and educates those who are not comfortable interacting with these communities because they are not themselves ace or aro and facilitates understanding, acceptance, and solidarity.

Quotes

The quotes we use throughout the book were collected using questionnaires. Everyone surveyed knew that we planned to use their quotes for this purpose and consented to this usage. They also picked the name they wished to be identified with. Beyond their name and comment, we gathered a small amount of demographic information. All people surveyed said they were 18 years or older.

These quotes were not collected as part of a research study, but rather were intended to serve as anecdotal evidence of some of the experiences that aro and ace people have, particularly to add perspectives that we as the authors do not have. They should not be generalized beyond illustrating the specific experiences of the individuals involved, which is also why we are not releasing any of the aggregated demographic data.

The quotes have been collected from aromantic and asexual individuals from all over the world, but the authors of this book are primarily familiar with Western and anglophone ace and aro communities. While we tried to ensure that all ace and aro perspectives were included, we recognize and acknowledge that we were not able to do so, and this book certainly does not adequately represent non-Western and non-anglophone communities. Aromantic and asexual people come from all walks of life, all races, ethnicities, disabilities, ages, genders, and backgrounds—no one book can completely represent all of those identities and perspectives, and we advise you to look for more information from other diverse sources to get a broader understanding of asexuality and aromanticism.

A Note on Terms

In this book, we explore the process of understanding and embracing an aromantic or asexual identity. We, as the authors of this book, all belong to ace or aro communities, and we are sharing stories and perspectives from ourselves and other aro and ace individuals. This means that we will be using the language of our communities. There is a comprehensive glossary at the end of this book with definitions of every term we think is relevant when interacting with aro and ace individuals. We will not be defining terms as they come up in this book except where necessary, and we encourage you to utilize our glossary as you read the book.

However, the definitions we provide in the glossary are only a starting point. For example, the term "asexual" is commonly defined as "feeling little to no sexual attraction" and the term "aromantic" is commonly defined as "feeling little to no romantic attraction," but neither is fully encapsulated by this definition, as there are many reasons people identify as aromantic or asexual beyond the dictionary definition—which we explain in more detail in Chapter 1 and explore in depth throughout the book.

Label Clarification

Many labels used by LGBTQIA+ people are extremely subjective and have specific meanings to each individual who uses them. That is just as true in aromantic and asexual communities, where people are constantly reinventing and redefining the vocabulary to describe their own orientations. We aim to define terms in this book in the most comprehensive of ways, but we recognize that different people will have different definitions and understandings of these terms. We do not deny the validity of other definitions—we aim to use the most general and up-to-date understanding of these words at the time of writing. Your own interpretation and understanding of the labels that you use for yourself takes precedence over anything we have to say about those labels.

When we use the term "ace" we are referring to anyone who identifies within the asexual community or on the asexual spectrum for any reason at all. When we use the term "asexual" when referring to a hypothetical person's identity, we are defining it as "experiencing no sexual attraction at all." However, the term "asexuality" generally refers to the orientation of feeling little to no sexual attraction. Some people within the ace community might identify as asexual while experiencing some level of sexual attraction, while others might not even know or understand what sexual attraction feels like and so not know if they feel it or not.

The same goes for aromanticism. When we use the term "aro" we are referring to anyone who identifies within the aromantic community or on the aromantic spectrum for any reason at all. When we use the term "aromantic" when referring to a hypothetical person's identity, we are defining it as "experiencing no romantic attraction at all." However, the term "aromanticism" refers to the orientation of feeling little to no romantic attraction. Some people within the aro community might identify as aromantic while experiencing some level of romantic attraction, while others may not even know or understand what romantic attraction feels like and so not know if they feel it or not.

When quoting a respondent, we always use the labels that they identify with. In general, always respect an individual's definition of themselves as whatever label they choose.

While we refer to grayromanticism and graysexuality as within the aromantic and asexual spectrums respectively, and also consider all microlabels we define in this book as being within the aro or ace communities, some people who identify with those microlabels do not identify with the aro or ace communities. For example, someone who identifies as demiromantic, meaning they do not experience romantic attraction until after they have already formed another kind of emotional bond with someone else, might not consider that identity significantly different from the experience of alloromantic people and thus may not identify as aromantic or part of the aro community. Similarly, many quoisexual people, who identify as not knowing or understanding sexual attraction, find the label asexual inaccurate, as it implies a certainty they do not have. Again, we always respect everyone's understanding of their own identity. The aro and ace communities tend to place a high value on the idea that people know their own orientations and identities best and are best equipped to say for themselves what communities they belong to. We believe that this is a good idea and should be standard in more than just the aro and ace communities.

Some aro and ace people identify as a part of the larger queer community; some do not, and do not feel included or want to be included by the acronym. We certainly consider the aro and ace communities as part of the LGBTQIA+ umbrella but, again, don't insist that all, or any, individuals who identify as ace or aro must identify as queer or as under that umbrella. Some ace and aro people identify as outside of the false binary of straight or LGBTQ+, and others identify with the label "queer" without identifying with the larger LGBTQ+ communities.

Also, there are many terms within the aro and ace communities that do not have universally agreed-upon spellings. In the glossary, we include all the spellings we know about, but we use one spelling simply to avoid confusion and remain consistent. Again, we are not endorsing any specific spelling or usage.

The Goals of This Book

This book is meant to be a gateway to understanding asexual and aromantic identity and community, in all of their variations, as well as the challenges aro and ace people often experience. This book is both a 101 and a 201, an explanation of "what" and "why." We do not try to define or specify what asexuality or aromanticism "should" look like; rather, we have written the book with the understanding that aromanticism and asexuality can manifest in many different ways for many different people while still being connected by some similar experiences.

For those who are questioning if they are ace or aro, this book may help you learn about a variety of labels under the aro and ace umbrellas, community history, challenges you may face, and ways to overcome those challenges. For those who know someone who is aro or ace, this book may help you better understand what they are going through, what their identity means to them, and how to support and advocate for them in different contexts. For those who are simply curious or thought the cover looked cool, this book may help you learn about the diversity of sexuality and orientation, how non-romantic and non-sexual identities can influence one's sexuality and orientation, and the challenges that people face, regardless of orientation, living in an allonormative and amatonormative world.

We include advice about how to handle some of the obstacles that come up in exploring an aro or ace identity, from processing the nuances of the identities, to joining a community, to coming out. This advice is from us, as people who have faced or are facing these challenges, to anyone who might be struggling—either you yourself, or your friends, family, patients, students, or anyone else you believe that you can help.

Lastly, we hope this book gets you thinking about sexuality, orientation, and identity. In writing this book, we worked to explore not only all of the things that impact our own personal identities, but also the things that don't impact us or that impact our peers more than ourselves. We have written this book as a reflection of the conversations and guidance we wish were more widely available to people questioning or coming to terms with their orientations and people looking to learn more about the ways that allonormativity and amatonormativity impact them.

CHAPTER 1

Basics

Asexuality and Aromanticism as Complex Identities

Reasons Someone Might Identify As Aro or Ace

There are many different reasons you or someone you know may identify with the ace or aro communities, and all are valid if the individual feels they are valid. Some, though certainly not all, of the reasons are listed below. We take a descriptivist perspective on labels rather than a prescriptivist perspective. This means that we do not believe in dictating how anyone should label themselves or their experiences, but rather, we seek to provide support for and information for your and others' personal journeys.

Also, someone can identify with the experiences described in this section but not with the label(s) often used for those experiences—for instance, an allosexual nonbinary person may have a very low libido, and while someone else with a very similar level of libido might identify as asexual or graysexual, fae might not feel connected with the label or the community. Whatever label fae uses is legitimate, and fae is the only person qualified to choose faer own identity. We encourage you to read these experiences with an open mind and consider how they may be different or similar to your own, and you are free to take or leave any labels that you discover.

LACK OF ATTRACTION (SEXUAL OR ROMANTIC)

The standard definitions for asexuality and aromanticism are based around attraction—asexuality is defined as "little to no sexual attraction," and aromanticism is defined as "little to no romantic attraction," and most communities revolve around this definition. In many ways, this is a very inclusive definition—it means that aro and ace orientations are not defined by action. If a gay man has sex with a woman despite not being attracted to her, he is still gay; so too can aromantic people engage in romances with others and still be aromantic if those romances are not based around romantic attraction.

> *"I have never had/felt sexual attraction to another human being, no matter the connection we have shared I have never looked at someone and felt the need to sleep with them. As an aro I don't experience much of a romantic attraction either, however I do sometimes drift off and wonder what it'd be like if someone gained a crush on me—a feeling that tend[s] to end as a thought and not much else."—Sara S*

However, this definition is only a starting point. For asexual and aromantic people who do not know what attraction feels like, this definition may not be useful, as they are not sure whether or not they have felt it before. Other aromantic and asexual people may conceptually understand attraction but define their orientation in a way that centers some other aspect of their experience.

LACK OF DESIRE TO ENGAGE IN SEX

Another perspective on asexuality focuses on desire, rather than attraction, as that might be an easier concept for people to grasp. While attraction and desire may be synonymous for some people, for others there is a clear distinction. Sexual attraction is a sensation or feeling that can be defined in different ways but is generally directed towards another person, feels sexual in some sense to the person experiencing it, and may or may not be connected to specific acts or fantasies. On the other hand, desire may be connected to acts or fantasies but not be tied to a specific other person. Someone can generally have a desire for a sex act that is unconnected to any individual person or people in general or may be generally averse to or repulsed by sex acts of all kinds regardless of the person.

This may be particularly relevant for graysexual, quoisexual, or demisexual people who feel attraction or desire under specific circumstances and who may not always be sure that what they feel is real—they can define their orientation by their desires to engage in sexual behavior rather than attraction towards specific people. Even if you do not identify as gray-, quoi-, or demi-, you still do not have to analyze or decipher whether or not you experience attraction if that does not serve you.

It should be noted that because of compulsory sexuality (the assumption and pressure for all people to desire and engage in sexual acts) even determining one's desire or lack thereof can be difficult as well. This is especially the case for groups who face additional pressure from their society to be sexual or are more frequently hypersexualized, such as Black men and Hispanic and Latina women.

> "I wasn't opposed to sex; I masturbated and felt things after reading or watching a sexy scene in fiction. I also wasn't opposed to romance; I loved a well-written love story and Taylor Swift was my favorite musician. I thought that being romance- and sex-favorable (terms I didn't know at the time) disqualified me from being aro or ace. I didn't start identifying on the ace spectrum until I learned that attraction and desire are not the same thing."—PJ

LACK OF INTEREST IN/INDIFFERENCE TO
ROMANCE AND ROMANTIC RELATIONSHIPS

A counterpart to the above focuses on the desire to engage in romantic relationships or romance. Amatonormativity is the assumption that everyone desires and should desire romance and that romantic relationships are the most important. However, despite what most media and our society says, some people do not find romantic relationships important to them, and they do not want to engage in romantic behaviors of any kind. Whether they have romantic feelings may be irrelevant, because again, not everyone can tell when feelings are romantic. While some people who do not want to be in a romantic relationship may be "not ready to settle down," others simply do not want to be in a romantic relationship at all. The assumption that they should pursue romantic relationships is an expression of amatonormativity in itself.

> *"I definitely was aro before I had a term to describe it. When my friends, when we were pre-teens and young teens, began to have crushes or 'fall in love,' I never did. I was never repulsed in any way by their 'puppy love,' and I was happy to talk about their crushes with them. I never felt the same way, though, and never really wanted to. I've always been a reader, and I identified, even as a kid, with writers and characters who remained single: Jane Austen, Harper Lee, Hercule Poirot, Thoreau, Isaac Newton (just a few, varied ones 😊)."—Brian F*

LACK OF IDENTIFICATION WITH ROMANCE AS
A RELEVANT RELATIONSHIP CATEGORY

While there is not universal agreement on what "counts" as sexual behavior, there is even less agreement on romantic behavior. You may have experienced or seen this in your own relationships, where you or people you know are assumed by others to be a romantic couple, but the people involved are engaging in behavior they consider platonic. What may seem like platonic group activities to one person will be romantic to another, like going out to dinner, cuddling, sharing feelings, or saying "I love you." Some people may choose to participate in all of those activities because they enjoy them and enjoy other people's company, but not classify those activities as romantic. These people may even engage in relationships that externally appear romantic and include signifiers that are traditionally attached to romantic commitments, such as cohabitation, sharing finances, and coparenting, but romance may not be a useful signifier for them.

> "I see my past self the same way I described myself, 'nothing.' I didn't feel like anything so I don't see my past self as anything. It's kind of confusing to explain but that's my best effort. I conceptualized it as an absence. Like trying to describe the color of air, there just isn't anything there."—Amber

LACK OF LIBIDO/PHYSICAL CAPABILITY

Some people identify as asexual because they physically do not have a sex drive. While that might be defined by some medical institutions as a deficit, it is not inherently bad or wrong to lack a libido—the only problem is if that lack causes distress. (Even then, it is important to distinguish between the distress that is internal and the distress that comes from not matching societal expectations.[1]) For this definition, it is particularly crucial to keep the next section in mind—orientations can shift for many reasons, including an increase or decrease in libido. It is possible to identify as asexual at one point in time due to a lack of sex drive, then experience a change and no longer identify as asexual. It is also possible to identify as asexual after a decrease in libido due to a number of factors. However, the assumption

---

1   See "Experiences with Low and Non-Existent Libido" in Chapter 6.

should always be that whatever libido someone has is fine for them as long as they are satisfied with it.

> *"Prior to identifying as ace, I conceptualized my identity as a temporary lack of libido due to my young age, gender identity (the stereotype that women are less sexual or that not enjoying sex as a woman is considered normal), or upbringing in which sexuality was not often spoken about."—Raphaëlle*

OTHERS NOT MENTIONED HERE

There are far more reasons than those listed here that people identify with the ace or aro labels or communities. As we discuss in Chapter 2, most of the aro and ace community development has been in Western countries, and the communities use primarily Western constructs to think about sexual and romantic orientations, in a way that many other cultures may not relate to. This means that there are some people who might relate to the experiences of aro or ace people without using the label themselves or may not think the label is relevant to their lives. We strongly believe in the importance of defining one's own identity and would never presume to tell another person how they should label themselves, but we also believe that the perspectives offered by this book can be useful beyond our communities alone and would recommend that anyone who reads it thinks about how it could apply to themselves or the people around them. There are also culturally specific labels, such as two-spirit, that can refer to orientation and that might be used in place of or in addition to "asexual" or "aromantic."

Anyone may also personally identify on the basis of more than one of these reasons. For example, one might lack romantic attraction and also not think of romance as a relevant category in their life, and define themself as aro because of both factors.

Models of Attraction and Orientation

Models of orientation categorize and describe orientation based on certain defining factors. The defining factors of a model are often limited to only one or two of the reasons described in the paragraphs above. The majority of models specifically focused on ace and aro orientations center attraction and also explain attraction in different ways.

Types of Attraction

Many models that ace and aro people use to define their identities also assume that there are different forms of attraction that people can feel. While there are many different kinds of attraction, and this list is certainly not exhaustive, the most commonly named ones in the Western English-speaking aro and ace communities are as follows.

- **Sexual attraction** is a pull towards a specific person that feels sexual or that leads to desire to engage in intimate physical or sexual contact with someone.
- **Romantic attraction** is an emotional form of attraction that is often separate from other emotional attractions and often leads to desire to engage in behaviors deemed romantic.
- **Platonic attraction** is the desire to engage in a type of non-romantic emotional relationship with a specific person, usually in the form of a friendship. Historically, while platonic relationships are often defined exclusively as non-sexual, in current aro communities platonic relationships can be either sexual or non-sexual.
- **Alterous attraction** is a newer term and thus does not have a solid definition, and while there are many arguable points about what it is, the communities

generally agree that it is a desire for some form of emotional closeness with a specific person that cannot solely be described as romantic or platonic.

- **Aesthetic attraction** is a sensory pull towards a specific person. It is usually visual but can also be auditory or olfactory, or relate to any of the other senses. However, tactile-related attraction is usually only classified under sensual attraction.
- **Sensual attraction** is a pull to engage in physical, non-sexual actions with a specific person, such as hugging, cuddling, or holding hands.
- **Noetic or intellectual attraction** is a pull focused on connecting with someone else's intellect, opinions, or knowledge. It can also focus on the desire to learn from someone, teach someone, become their mentor, or form a connection with a mind that functions similarly to one's own.

Some people experience many other specific forms of attraction; conversely, many of these are not distinct for everyone, and the definitions we provide are certainly not universal. Most aro or ace people specifically define their romantic or sexual attractions, as that often defines their orientation. Similar to sexual and romantic attraction, other attractions may be gender-based and may be how one identifies their orientation, such as homoplatonic or panalterous. People can also specifically identify on a sliding scale with any attraction, including identifying as demisensual, aplatonic, or grayaesthetic.

We discuss some well-known models of attraction and orientation below. None of these are perfect, and some are considered by many to be incredibly flawed. However, they are worth discussing because some of these models are used by researchers and theorists to discuss and understand orientations including asexuality and aromanticism. Additionally, some people may find a particular model to be really helpful in their own understanding of their own orientation.

Kinsey Scale

Alfred Kinsey interviewed more than 8000 individuals during his research over the course of the 1940s and into the 1950s and rated individuals on a scale of 0 for "Exclusively heterosexual" to 6 for "Exclusively homosexual." He acknowledged publicly in his research that not all individuals interviewed fit nicely on his 0 to 6 scale, and he assigned these individuals to a Group X for those who had "No socio-sexual contacts or reactions." This was a behavior-based model and would not account for many of those who identify as asexual today, but it was one of the earliest published acknowledgements that not everyone fits on a scale of heterosexual to homosexual and one of the earliest acknowledgements that some people have no sexual attraction or interest in others.

Storms' Model

One of the first models to explicitly include asexuality is from Michael Storms' "Theories of Sexual Orientation" published in 1980, which was intended to update Kinsey's scale by placing hetero- and homo-eroticism as axes on a graph.[2] According to this model, someone with high homo-eroticism and low hetero-eroticism is homosexual, someone with high hetero-eroticism and low homo-eroticism is heterosexual, someone with high homo-eroticism and hetero-eroticism is bisexual, and someone with low homo-eroticism and hetero-eroticism is asexual.

This model is oversimplified, as it is predicated on a gender binary that many people do not subscribe to or believe in, does

2   Storms, M. D. (1980) "Theories of sexual orientation." *Journal of Personality and Social Psychology 38*, 783–792.

not address romantic attraction at all, and presumes that eroticism is identical to sexuality or attraction. However, it does define asexuality in a way that many people agree with—low or no sexual (or erotic) attraction to any gender at all, though as we explained above, asexuality can be more complex than that.

The expectation was and is that romantic and sexual attractions, and any other possible attractions, all align in any and every case of attraction. This model represents that by only defining orientations by eroticism. The implication is both that any other attraction feelings will align with one's erotic attraction and that erotic attraction is more significant or possibly precursory to other attractions.

There is still a widespread social norm for words like "heterosexual" or "homosexual" to be assumed to include both sexual and romantic aspects of behavior, even when using these more technical, scientific terms instead of the broader "straight" or "gay." In fact, "sexual orientation" as a category is assumed by most of society to include romantic preference and leanings, as well as other forms of attraction.

Split Attraction Model (SAM)

The Split Attraction Model generally refers to the idea that people can and often do differentiate, or "split," the kinds of attraction they feel and do not feel, defined above in "Types of Attraction." Not everyone who can or does experience these attractions differently uses or identifies with the SAM.

There is some controversy around the use of the SAM. Many ace individuals resent being asked their romantic orientation as well, as they feel "asexual" summarizes their identity. On the other hand, many aro people are frustrated by the way that asexuality and sexual orientation generally seem to be emphasized over aromanticism and romantic orientation. Others feel that the term "split" characterizes their attractions as not whole or somehow "less than." Additionally, some people don't feel that they can distinguish between different forms of attraction, and the insistence that they should causes them anxiety or discomfort.

The naming and use of the model conflates attraction and orientation. This does not work for people who identify with orientations for other reasons—for example, some people identify as asexual because they are heavily sex-repulsed and not because they feel little to no sexual attraction. Therefore, despite the name, the SAM is often used to describe split orientations regardless of whether or not the orientation is specifically attraction based. Finally, the SAM is often used to discuss exclusively romantic and sexual orientations, and those who identify with and prioritize other orientations feel unrepresented by the most common uses of the SAM.

In general, ace people can have any romantic (or other) orientation and aro people can have any sexual (or other) orientation, but not all of them choose to distinguish those orientations as different, and not all who do differentiate them view that as being part of the SAM.

Primary and Secondary Attraction Model
Another model occasionally used in asexual communities is called the Primary and Secondary Attraction Model. According to this model, "primary" attraction is a type that may be felt immediately upon seeing or meeting someone. Primary attraction is often towards aesthetic appearances. There are also some traits connected to personality and emotional connection, and attraction based on those traits is called "secondary." This model was intended to help explain how sexual attraction functioned for demisexual people, who could use it to express how they develop sexual attraction based on secondary traits rather than primary traits. This model was inspired by a post

from an Asexual Visibility and Education Network (AVEN)[3] forum member called Rabger and was originally called "Rabger's Model," from 2006 to 2011, until Rabger clarified that it was significantly different from their ideas.

This model has some issues as well, as it is interpreted very differently by different people. Some say that it should only be applied to sexual attraction, while others feel that they can experience any of the different attraction types based on primary or secondary traits. Many people also feel this model doesn't accurately distinguish the difference between how demi people experience attraction and how allo people experience attraction. Also, some people believe that the labels "primary" and "secondary" place attraction types in a hierarchy unnecessarily and that they can feel attraction immediately based on traits classified as "secondary." Others see it as needlessly confusing.

Other

There are a variety of other models of attraction and orientation. Above, we have covered the ones that are most well known in the ace and aro communities, although not always well known for good reasons. Other models, such as the Attraction Layer Cake, radar charts, and the Genderbread Person or Gender Unicorn,[4] similarly have pros and cons. A problem that many models share is that they fail to account for many genders, orientations, and types of attraction, often by not having enough nuance and presenting only a few concrete options.

Orientations are Fluid

It is possible for orientations to naturally change over time. For example, someone might identify (correctly) as bisexual

---

3   For more about AVEN, see "Community History" in Chapter 2.

4   For more on these models, see https://asexualagenda.wordpress. com/2019/04/30/terrible-graphs-of-orientation. Accessed on 19/9/2022.

during their adolescence and early twenties and yet in their late twenties start experiencing a persistent apathy towards the idea of dating and romantic relationships. This person might later come to identify as aromantic as well as bisexual, but before they understand what is going on, they will experience these feelings of confusion. For people who have this kind of experience, the confusion and sense of difference can be in comparison to their previous orientation as well as the new one.

Sometimes the previous understanding of identity was not incorrect; it was merely incomplete, because of the possibilities for grayness in each spectrum, and because of the possibility that people have different sexual and romantic orientations. People might have been accurate in their description of the genders to whom they are attracted but realize that that attraction is not both sexual and romantic (or even that it is neither sexual nor romantic!). Later, with more information and understanding, people might add an aro or ace label to the identity they already had.

With increased understanding, people often change the ways they describe themselves. Naturally, people's use of labels to describe themselves changes with their understanding of self. It is well documented that many change the ways in which they label their orientation over time. Many incorrectly assume complete immutability regarding descriptions of sexual and romantic orientation—that is, that when one first declares an identity, it must remain fixed for life—and this misconception certainly applies to the aromantic and asexual spectrums. Some assume that the use of a past orientation label, such as gay or bisexual, to describe oneself permanently overrides an emerging concept of oneself as a person on the asexual or aromantic spectrum, or vice versa (note that this assumption also occurs when someone previously identified as straight but it is exacerbated by having prior queer orientations and labels). Some assume that the state of identifying on the asexual or aromantic spectrum is always temporary and that these communities consist primarily of "late bloomers." Many underestimate the extent to which most people, especially those who do not identify as heterosexual and heteroromantic, instinctually understand their sexual and romantic preferences and how early these instincts may surface, even if someone lacks words to describe them. Given the current scarcity of information and resources pertaining to aromanticism and asexuality, it is understandable that one may only arrive upon a descriptor under one, or perhaps both, of these umbrellas after first identifying with a more mainstream label.

> "I think everyone who IDs as asexual or/and aromantic wonder[s] if they're just faking it or if they'll eventually end up liking someone in that regard. It was only when I started accepting that this is 'me' at this point in my life. All identities are fluid, it took me a few years to eventually get to this point of acceptance, and if I do end up changing, then at least I have a better understanding of myself." —Anon.

If you do not yet identify as ace or aro, but are questioning whether these labels might be useful for you, it may be helpful to understand some of the ways people who currently identify as asexual or aromantic felt prior to identifying that way themselves. You may connect with one or more of these situations, but even if you don't, we hope that these examples are reassuring because they can demonstrate the fluidity of orientations. Broadly, there are three main situations ace and aro people might have been in if they identified as another orientation before identifying as ace or aro.

- They identified with something else either because they had not heard of asexuality or aromanticism before, or because when they first heard about asexuality or aromanticism they didn't yet understand the range of experiences the orientations capture and dismissed the possibility that either of those terms could describe them.

- They didn't actively identify as any orientation at all until they found asexuality or aromanticism but rather spent years of their adolescence or even their adulthood not having access to the orientation label(s) that they later realized applied to them all along. Those people might have identified with a description such as "late bloomer" rather than an orientation at all.
- They previously identified their romantic or sexual orientation accurately but then experienced a shift in their orientation.

Below are a few hypothetical examples demonstrating how people might change how they identify over time. These examples are inspired by the experiences of aro and ace people in the questionnaires.

- A 14-year-old boy who identifies as gay might later, once discovering more about the ace and aro spectrums, realize he is homoromantic and asexual. He might choose at age 18 to call himself a gay ace.
- A nonbinary person who identifies as bisexual in college might later realize that their bisexual identity does not include romantic attraction as it does for many alloromantic bisexual people. In their late twenties, they might start identifying as aromantic bisexual.
- A woman who had always identified as straight figured out in her late twenties she was bisexual, after becoming attracted to a close female friend. Then, in her forties, she discovered demisexuality and realized that

it described her experiences. She noticed that she also experienced romantic attraction in a way that could be called biromantic and demiromantic, but since these identities matched her sexual orientation, she was content with just identifying as demisexual and bisexual.

Many other people consider their previous identity labels to have been inaccurate. However, it is always up to the person themselves to decide if any previous orientation labels were incorrect. Someone can consider their previous orientation as accurate and their newly discovered aro or ace identification as a modification or clarification of their previous identity. Either view is valid reasoning to a newly identifying ace and/or aro person.

In some cases when a person experiences a shift away from a different orientation, it might occur after a traumatic event. One such example is a person who does not feel any sexual attraction after a sexual assault and chooses an ace identity label to better describe how entirely differently they feel towards their sexual orientation going forward. A shift to feeling that an ace orientation now fits better than a previously used sexual orientation can also occasionally occur after a physical yet permanent change in libido, such as because of a new medication one intends to stick with for the remainder of their life (or a significant period of the future) but which dramatically decreased their sex drive. It is also legitimate to disconnect from romantic attraction or the idea of a romantic relationship after a traumatic or abusive relationship. Any of these shifts could be temporary or permanent, but if the label "aro" or "ace" feels relevant, it should be respected as such.[5]

Regardless of whether the cause of the change is one of the aforementioned reasons, another reason, or entirely unknown,

---

5 For more, see "History of Trauma" in Chapter 6.

a shift in orientation should always be respected as a person's description of their current internal perceptions. It does not need to be historically consistent within the person for it to be accurate for how they feel they are in the present and going forward. The vast majority of people we surveyed for this book reported that they always had been aro, ace, or both, even when they did not fully understand themselves. Many of the responses discussed believing they had not yet met the right person, whether ace or aro—this messaging is the only way many people had to frame their life experiences. Later, we will discuss the prevalence of these messages and how they impact everyone, including allo people.[6] However, the ace and aro communities can provide a haven from this messaging and a safe place for imagining an aro or ace future.

---

6   See "Compulsory Sexuality" and "Amatonormativity" in Chapter 6.

* CHAPTER 2 *

Community History and Culture

Community History

If you are ace or aro, you are not alone—you have never been alone. Aro and ace people have always existed. Long before the internet, long before people coalesced around specific terminology and labels, individual people came up with their own ways of describing their orientations and experiences. Some of them went through similar processes of understanding and accepting their identities, even without the resources available today. Others struggled to understand their orientations because the concepts were not available in their societies. Ace and aro communities existed, too, out of the spotlight and within other queer communities. As a result of this obscurity and the lack of standard terminology, much aro and ace history has been lost to time. We hope that people uncover more about asexual and aromantic history—we're confident there's lots to learn.

Modern ace and aro communities only date back about two decades, since they were able to connect via modern technology. The youth of these communities has had a profound impact on the recognition of our identities and the issues that aromantic and asexual people face.

While there are some historical mentions of experiences resembling what people today call asexuality and aromanticism, sustained communities only emerged with the beginnings of the internet. Although other LGBTQ+ communities were active and organizing throughout the last century and beyond, lasting ace and aro communities didn't develop in the same way. There are no records that strongly indicate a sustained asexual community before the internet existed, although it is possible that they did exist. Various snippets of newspaper article and write-in advice columns show that people did use the word "asexual" similarly to the modern usage well before the age of the internet. No historical record exists, as far as we know, for the term "aromantic." Similar terms, such as "non-limerant" and "anaphrodite," existed for describing experiences that may have been referred to as asexual or aromantic in contemporary times.[1]

The bisexual community also acted as a home for many asexual and aromantic people. One possible reason is that bisexuality is generally defined as a similar attraction to all or more than one gender, and most aro and ace people have similar attraction to all or most genders—it just happens to be nil. Also, bisexuality used to be much more generally defined as "not gay and not straight,"[2] which also includes ace and aro people. (For a similar reason, many ace and aro people identify as bi or pan before they identify as ace or aro.)

> "Maybe I was bisexual? It would explain why I looked at men's and women's bodies equally, right? So for a time—though I was in high school so I didn't really research it much—I thought I was bisexual and told people so when they asked."—Telperion

One of the possible reasons communities struggled to rise is because asexual and aromantic identities revolve around a

---

1   See the Appendix for more resources that explore aro and ace history.
2   Newsweek Staff (1995) "Bisexuality." *Newsweek.* Accessed on 4/5/2022 at www.newsweek.com/bisexuality-184830.

lack of experience, and it can be hard to pinpoint what one isn't experiencing without the language to describe what that experience is. While gay people can recognize their attraction is simply pointed at a different gender than it is for straight people, aces might never realize what is different about them because they might not understand what sexual attraction is, and aros similarly might not understand what romantic attraction is and therefore struggle to identify a lack of it.

The terms modern ace and aro communities use to talk about attraction did not exist, or at least weren't common, in the 20th century and still aren't universal today. As a result, most asexuals and aromantics, at the time of writing, still discover their identity after reading about it online or hearing about it through word of mouth rather than on their own by recognizing their experiences as different from others' or recognizing themselves in concepts that are well known in society.

What is generally considered the first online ace community formed in the comments section of an article called "My Life as an Amoeba,"[3] a 1997 essay by someone named Zoe who talked about her experience as someone who identifies as asexual. (The symbol of the amoeba became an in-joke among asexuals, because they're an agametically, previously called asexually, reproducing organism.) The early internet site where the article was published allowed for comments, and people used the comments section to share their stories and discuss their experiences.

In 2000, an ace community started to emerge on a new Yahoo email group called "Haven for the Human Amoeba." Every month or so, a new person would leave some kind of introductory post, sparking a new discussion. This email group became the home

---

3   O'Reilly, Z. (1997) "My Life as an Amoeba." *StarNet Dispatches*. Accessed on 4/5/2022 at http://web.archive.org/web/20030210212218/http://dispatches.azstarnet.com/zoe/amoeba.htm.

to the early online community. Many concepts and much terminology central to asexuality sprouted from this era.

The first known usage of the term "aromantic" as it is used today was posted on Haven for the Human Amoeba in 2002. The ace and aro communities have shared origins and many shared experiences, and together comprise the aspec community[4] as a whole. More recently, the aro community has become more developed as its own community, as many ace individuals are not aro and many aro individuals are not ace. However, the above quote documents the fact that aros who were either not ace or "not quite" ace were part of the modern aro and ace communities' beginnings even before they had the words to talk about aromanticism.

In 2001, the Asexual Visibility and Education Network—also known as AVEN—was founded by David Jay. It had two main goals: 1) to help the public learn about asexuality and have a place to share their questions; 2) to provide an online forum to foster asexual community growth through the process of asexual individuals sharing about their experiences. When AVEN started hosting forums in 2002, the site for years became the main online hub for the ace community. The English language forum has over 142,000 members at the time of writing.

Asexual Awareness Week, as it was originally called, takes place the last full week in October and was established in 2010 by Sara Beth Brooks with the goal of spreading awareness about asexuality, as it was, and largely still is, a lesser-known orientation.[5] To this end, the Asexual Awareness Week team organized events, both in person and online, created educational

---

4   "Aspec" is a term that refers to the entire community of aro and ace people. We have chosen not to use this term throughout this book. However, the term "aspec" represents the fact that many people do consider all ace and aro people to be part of one big community.

5   Asexual Outreach, Inc (2020) "The History of Ace Week." Accessed on 24/5/2022 at www.aceweek.org/the-history-of-ace-week.

materials, and discussed asexual experiences. In 2019, Asexual Outreach took over organizing the week and officially changed the name to Ace Week, because as societal visibility of asexual identities improved over the years, the goals of the week became broader than awareness, and people had begun campaigning for broader asexual acceptance and celebrating asexual pride during the week.

The Asexual Awareness Week Community Census was created by the Asexual Awareness Week team in 2011 in order to gather data on the demographics of ace people. For example, there were questions about one's religious identity, one's asexual identity, and what online community spaces one frequented. Inspired by this, the AVEN Community Census was launched in 2014 by the AVEN Survey Team, and was created to obtain better data on the makeup of asexual communities and track trends over time. At the time it was collected in 2014, with 10,880 ace people surveyed, it was the largest-known dataset on the subject of asexuality to date. In 2017, the census began to be run by its own volunteer team, and in 2019 the name was changed to the Ace Community Survey, which is the current name at the time of writing.

The forum AroPlane began in 2012 and was created specifically for aromantic people regardless of sexual identity. AroPlane was short lived, and Arocalypse soon took its place in 2013 as the main forum for aromantic people to engage in. Arocalypse has 2912 members at the time of writing.

Aromantic Spectrum Awareness Week, or ASAW, originally called Aromantic Awareness Week, was first celebrated November 10–17, 2014. The name change occurred in 2015 along with a change in the dates from November to the first full week after Valentine's Day.[6] There was a poll spread through Tumblr's

---

6 ASAW (n.d.) "About ASAW." Accessed on 24/5/2022 at www.arospecweek. org/about-asaw.

aromantic communities to decide this name change. ASAW has events, social challenges, and prompts. All of this is a joint project currently managed by Aromantic-Official, AUREA, and other members of the aromantic communities. Some aromantic people and organizations not directly affiliated with the ASAW team also create their own events, prompts, and other community and activist projects during ASAW.

Today, there are aro and ace communities on most social media platforms.[7]

> *"[During] Aromantic Spectrum Awareness Week [in] my first year of university, I was determined to raise awareness. Through the university's pride center, I bought aro chocolate bars and made pamphlets to give out. It was just me, some black and white pamphlets, and a bowl of chocolate at a table until my aromantic friend came to take my place two hours later."—Lindsay*

Aro and Ace Culture

There are numerous ways people engage in ace and aro culture, many of which help them feel bonded to their communities. This section discusses anglophone aro and ace communities.[8]

Ace and Aro Flags

Like most identities within the LGBTQIA+ community, there is a flag associated with asexuality and another associated with aromanticism. The asexual flag was invented by AVEN forum user standup in 2010, and after it was chosen as the community flag by a vote on the AVEN forums, it spread to other spaces of

---

7   For a longer list of social media communities, see "Online," "Asexual/ Aromantic Communities" in Chapter 7.
8   See "Quotes" in Introduction for more information.

the ace community. The ace flag consists of four stripes: from top to bottom, black, gray, white, and purple. The black, gray, and white represent the spectrum of sexuality: black for asexuals, the gray specifically representing anyone with a graysexual identity including demisexuals, and white for allosexuals. The purple represents community, and was chosen because it was already an accent color on AVEN.

The current aromantic flag was created by cameronwhimsy on Tumblr in 2014, and consists of five stripes, from top to bottom: dark green, light green, white, gray, and black. The two green stripes represent the different aro identities; green was chosen because it is the opposite of red, often representing romance, on a color wheel. White represents platonic and aesthetic attraction, as well as platonic relationships. Gray represents anyone who identifies with a grayromantic identity, and black represents the spectrum of sexuality, as there are aromantic people who identify with every sexual orientation.

There are also many flags for microlabels associated with the ace and aro communities. Many of them utilize similar color schemes to the ace and aro flags. Several of these microlabels are in our glossary.

Colors
Based in large part on the flags, the colors associated with asexuality and aromanticism respectively are purple and green, and these colors show up in most aro and ace community spaces.

Ace Ring and Aro Ring
Many asexual people wear a black ring on the middle finger of their right hand to symbolize their connection to their ace identity and community, a trend that started on the AVEN forums in 2005. It can serve as a way to identify publicly without being out or as an alternative to a wedding band. While most are plain

black, some people's rings are also purple or gray, or include designs from card suits.

> *"I have an intense connection to my ring. [...] Not everyone, okay, most people, don't even know it's an ace ring. But I do. It's a public display of my identity that only those who also identify or are allies know, so it's sorta like a secret code that makes me happy. I don't want to hide who I am, what I am, but I don't also want to announce it to clueless people. This is a great compromise."*—Jenny J

The aro ring is white or silver and is worn on the middle finger of the left hand. Similar to the ace ring, it symbolizes a connection to the aromantic community and serves as a way to express pride in one's identity. Some people might also wear green or green and white rings or rings with arrow or spade designs.

> *"I do wear two rings that together make up the colors of the aro flag, because I like to broadcast it in a subtle way for people who might recognize what it means."*—Angel

Spades, Arrows, Cake, Dragons, and More

Similar to how in wider society heart symbols often represent romance, the heart symbol is also commonly used in the ace and aro communities to represent romantic orientation. It was common for a time to add a heart in a different pride flag's colors over the asexual flag to represent the ace person's romantic orientation.

There are many other symbols in aro and ace communities, most of which stem from community in-jokes. Because the abbreviation for asexual is ace, spelled and pronounced the same as the playing card, some people use the card suits to specify their identity. While there are a variety of intricacies to the usage of card suits, the most well-known usage is the spade or ace of spades, commonly used to represent asexuals and more commonly aromantic asexuals. The spade, independent of the ace, is also used more broadly to represent aromanticism, because the spade is seen as the opposite of a heart, as it resembles an inverted black heart.

> *"I got a spade tattoo as my first tattoo on my wrist, which has prompted many discussions."—Caroline S*

As the abbreviation for aromantic, "aro," is phonetically similar or identical to "arrow," depending on dialect, arrows are often used to symbolize aromanticism.

There is a common joke among asexuals based on the idea that "Cake is better than sex," so cake is another in-joke among ace individuals. Because some asexual people don't enjoy cake, garlic bread is also used. Space and space aesthetics are considered ace because space can be purple colored (such as certain nebulae) and because it includes the word "ace" within it. (Aro and ace communities are fond of puns.)

Dragons are often used to represent both ace and aro communities. This is at least in part due to the fact that the ace community has a strong existence in fandom spaces online and the characterization of Charlie Weasley from Harry Potter, who is fond of dragons and not very fond of other people in romantic or sexual ways. Also, it's a fun trivia fact that the Komodo dragon has been found to occasionally be able to reproduce agametically by parthenogenesis. As a counterpart to dragons, gryphons have been adopted as a specifically aro symbol, as have frogs, due to many frogs being green.

Voidpunk and Otherkin

Voidpunk is an identity for people who face dehumanization by society, including but not limited to ace and aro people, disabled people, neurodivergent people, and people of color. Voidpunk reclaims that dehumanization, recognizing that "human" is in many ways a socially constructed standard and rejecting it as valuable or meaningful to strive for. It was created by an allosexual aromantic person in response to being frequently dehumanized. The identity is usually expressed through an aesthetic, often creating a "voidsona" based on non-human beings, including aliens, robots, cryptids, eldritch beings, and abstract concepts. Voidpunk can also be an adjective applied to concepts that seem to align with the philosophy of reclaiming dehumanization.

Otherkin is an umbrella term for people who identify in some way as non-human entities, such as wolves, fae, or mythical creatures. These people may feel that they are spiritually these beings or that they were these beings in a past life. While voidpunk was created more recently, otherkin and similar identities, such as therian, have existed for at least two decades.

While not inherently part of aro or ace communities, ace and aro people may feel a connection to otherkin or voidpunk identities because of the dehumanization they often experience. See the Appendix for more resources on these identities.

Aro and Ace Representation in Media

Representation in books, TV, film, and other media has the potential to be a channel for greater awareness of asexuality and aromanticism. This potential is only starting to be realized. Historically, media lacked any acknowledgement of asexuality or aromanticism. Some aro and ace people interpreted certain fictional characters as being aro or ace even though the character's orientation is typically ambiguous. One well-known example of this is the character of Sherlock Holmes. Non-canonically ace and aro characters, as well as infamously poor canonical representation, became widely known points of connection within the communities.

In the past decade, ace and aro representation has started to grow—in books, movies, TV, video games, podcasts, and other forms of media. Increasingly, there is more visibility of asexuality and aromanticism, and much of this visibility is due to aro and ace creators making their own representation.[9] A few examples of positive media representation are the 2014–2020 TV show *BoJack Horseman* (a heteroromantic ace character), the 2015–2017 comic series *Jughead* (explicitly ace and implied aro main character), the 2018 young adult romance novel *Let's Talk About Love* by Claire Kann (a heteroromantic ace main character), and the 2020 young adult book *Loveless* by Alice Oseman (an aroace main character and other ace and aro side characters). Representations like these make aro and ace people feel seen and validated, and they provide opportunities for connection and bonding within the communities. They are often met with great excitement and strong engagement. Additionally, ace and aro people are excited to see themselves represented in the mainstream because these pieces of media can educate others about aromanticism and asexuality and provide visibility for the communities among the allo majority.

> *"I have wished I was 'normal' and struggled to feel whole as an asexual person. I respond to that by reading books with asexual characters written by asexual people."*—Cha Cha

However, this progress is slow and inconsistent. While there have been a small number of significant canonically ace characters in mainstream media, there have been almost no

---

9   There is a full database of published works featuring asexual or aromantic characters called The AroAce Database, created and maintained by Claudie Arseneault, herself an aroace author. In the Appendix, you can find a link to this database. The Appendix also includes an extensive list of examples of ace and aro media (including creators, activists, and advocates to follow).

canonically aro characters. Additionally, aside from the examples above and in the Appendix, the little representation that exists is often not accurate or even harmful. While this book is not predominantly about this topic, below is a short list of some common pitfalls that contribute to harmful and inaccurate aro or ace representation.

- Overemphasizing that asexual people can be alloromantic as a way to humanize them and further dehumanizing aromantic people in the process.
- Asexuality being represented as lack of interest in romance or romance-repulsion instead of mentioning the existence of aromanticism.
- Conflating aromanticism or asexuality with childishness and immaturity.
- Conflating asexuality or aromanticism with being cold and robotic.
- Coding only villains as allosexual and aromantic, to emphasize cruel "heartlessness" and demonize enjoying sex without certain types of emotions, instead of acknowledging good people can also be allosexual and aromantic.
- Providing a definition of asexuality or aromanticism that is misinformed, oversimplified, incomplete, or stereotypical.
- Depicting only aro or ace characters who are not human.
- Portraying being ace or aro as a phase, or depicting an aro or ace character becoming allo when they meet the "right" person.
- Avoiding labeling the character as canonically aro or ace.
- Identifying the character as ace or aro only in materials external to the content (such as in author interviews), not within the content itself.

- Only including aro and ace characters who are white, nondisabled, and cisgender, and generally failing to represent the full diversity of aro and ace people.

"I didn't really know what aro/ace was before so I don't think I even noticed any portrayals in media. But I definitely dislike it now! I wish they wouldn't make us seem so cold, detached from society and childish."—Luiza

Aside from professionally created works, many ace and aro people also find a great deal of joy in creating their own ace and aro characters in less formal settings, either by posting stories or videos featuring ace and aro original characters or creating transformative works, such as fanfiction. There are also fan cultures around aro and ace representation (both canonical and non-canonical) within the communities, and ace and aro creators make content like fanvids within these fandoms. Aro and ace individuals have also created small aro- or ace-themed zines, posted video essays, and used ace or aro pride flag colors to create impressive original artwork. All in all, the ace and aro communities value representation; even as the mainstream media lags behind, aro and ace people bring our representation into existence.

"I express my pride mainly online by creating stories with ace and aro characters in them to put a bit of myself in them and in the hope that if someone who felt like I did saw them they wouldn't feel so alone."—Amber

Current Community Dynamics
Within Ace and Aro Communities
While social media creates valuable opportunities for people to connect with each other, it unfortunately also opens space for

vitriol and divisiveness—both between different communities and within individual communities. As the aro and ace communities have large presences on social media, they are particularly vulnerable to these dynamics.

Some of the issues that plague aro and ace communities are ones that plague basically every community—racism, ableism, transphobia, misogyny, and other issues that arise when a certain space is dominated by a group with a certain privilege. The racism in particular is exacerbated because some of the most prominent voices in aro and ace communities are white, and many of the communities themselves are either dominated by or perceived to be dominated by white people.

Other issues are various forms of exclusionism and gate-keeping that are unique to the ace and aro communities. Individual aro and ace people have varying opinions on what makes someone aromantic or asexual. It is common for certain experiences to be pushed out of the community—specifically gray and demi orientations. This has been true from the beginning of ace and aro communities. When Haven for the Human Amoeba began, members were concerned with making sure only "true" asexuals were included and even presented new members with quizzes to ensure that they did not experience any attraction.[10] AVEN was started, at least in part, to be a more inclusionist space, but many members of the forums consistently disagree with allowing people to identify as asexual if they experience any level of sexual attraction. Even the header on the AVEN website itself has gone back and forth between defining asexuality as "experiencing no sexual attraction" and "experiencing little to no sexual attraction"—one definition is obviously much more inclusive than the other. The same can

---

10 AVEN Livestreams (2021) "Updating the Definition on the AVEN Home-page." Accessed on 24/5/2022 at www.youtube.com/watch?v=EouWUlU5 FnM.

be seen in many aromantic spaces as well, but with levels of romantic attraction.

Beyond that, there is often respectability politics at play, which can lead to some parts of the community being disrespected or overlooked. For example, alloromantic asexual people often say things like "Aces can still feel love," predicating acceptance on the idea of love, which ignores the needs of many aromantic people who don't connect with the word or concept of "love," particularly romantic love. At the same time, some aces are frustrated with feeling a responsibility to include aromanticism even if that isn't their identity or goal.

> *"Figuring out I was aro was definitely more difficult [than identifying as ace], because there are a lot less resources and a lot of ace resources are lowkey arophobic, emphasizing how being asexual doesn't mean being aro, and subconsciously saying how aces are still human since they're able to fall in love. There is a lot of amatonormativity in the ace community, and it makes it difficult questioning and identifying as aro."—Irene*

Exclusionist arguments in the ace and aro communities look similar to exclusionist arguments in other queer communities. Common exclusionist talking points are listed below.

- That certain experiences being included under a label "dilutes" the label or skews its meaning.
- That certain people using the label are doing so because it's "trendy," because they "want to be oppressed," or for some other disingenuous reason.
- That certain people in the community are ruining community spaces for others who say that they have a more legitimate claim to that identity.
- That certain groups or individuals who have "invaded"

the communities do not truly belong in the communities and that their presence inherently makes community spaces less safe for those who do "truly belong."

- That certain identities are a threat, possibly because these identities are seen as predatory, "stealing" resources, or "confusing" people outside of the community as to what the label or orientation "really" means.
- That ace and aro refer only to "attraction" or only to "desire" or only to "action," and using any other indicator or definition makes the identities meaningless.

Unfortunately, many of these talking points cycle through various community spaces and are aimed at a variety of people. People who are graysexual and grayromantic, demisexual and demiromantic, alloaro, sex-favorable aces, and romance-favorable aros tend to be the most common targets. These arguments will appear in community spaces and then often reappear cyclically, even if they have already been refuted, possibly many times over.

Within the Broader Queer Community
INCLUSION

Many aro and ace individuals consider themselves part of the greater LGBTQIA+ community. In the 2019 Ace Community Survey, 65.5 percent of aces considered themselves queer. Some aro or ace people have multiple orientation or gender labels that would qualify as LGBTQIA+, but many others identify as queer or LGBTQIA+ solely because of their ace or aro identity.

The majority of LGBTQIA+ organizations and communities are affirming and inclusive of asexual and aromantic identities and individuals, even if they often still have much to learn about how to best support and include us fully. Regardless, some of our best allies are often allo queer people.

"[I]n general I see overwhelming support from other members of the LGBTQ+ community and I feel worthy of identifying as 'queer.'"—Erin V

Even if they include aro and ace identities generally, LGBTQIA+ people and organizations sometimes use rhetoric that leaves us out, to our frustration and anger. For example, a common rallying cry of queer communities is "Love is Love," meaning that queer people should be accepted because their love, or romantic or sexual attraction to their partners, is as legitimate as non-queer people's love. This can make it seem like love is what "redeems" queer people or allows them to be accepted in mainstream society, as it theoretically bridges the difference between queer people and non-queer people. However, this framing obviously excludes ace or aro people.

"Generally, queer positivity is often about 'being allowed to love who you love' and as someone who doesn't love anyone romantically, I do feel removed from this a lot."—Sara

DISCOURSE

On the other hand, some queer people are exclusionary and purposefully leave aro and ace individuals and identities out of the queer community. These hate campaigns against aros and aces are most often referred to as "the discourse," also known as "discourse" or "ace discourse." "The discourse" has had multiple phases: its first intense stage occurred around the year 2011 on Tumblr, and another intense phase on Tumblr occurred in 2015. Now, waves of "discourse" are less common, as it has unfortunately become a constant in most online spaces, albeit less intense and pronounced. Much of "the discourse" centers on asexual people, as many of the aggressors involved either do not know of aromanticism or do not acknowledge it as an orientation.

"Honestly, I don't feel part of the LGBT community. There's so much hate against us and so many exclusionists that are just so goddamn loud."—Galli

Some features of "the discourse" are:

- people creating sideblogs to specifically target and harass ace and aro people
- taking pride in identifying as an "aphobe"
- memes that characterize asexuals as childish, similar to "special snowflake liberal" memes
- accusations towards the ace community, often that ace people are homophobic or sex-negative or that they inherently cause negativity and arguing in otherwise safe spaces
- vitriol towards asexuals that center on them existing, participating in LGBTQIA+ spaces, or engaging in/ showing pride. This can occur through direct messages and replies on posts
- saying that queerness is based specifically on oppression and believing that ace and aro people do not experience oppression and therefore do not belong in LGBTQIA+ communities
- accusations that aro or ace people are "stealing" resources from "real" queer people
- claiming that the "A" stands for ally—this may be intentional to discount ace and aro people or may be an unintentional slight.

This discourse often uses rhetoric that has been aimed at other niches of the LGBTQ+ community—that the people being discussed are attention seeking, lying, "actually straight," causing harm to others in the community, negatively affecting children, etc.

Many people in the ace and aro communities have negative associations with online spaces and arguments due to their experiences with "the discourse." Aro and ace bloggers became notably harder to find after the first several major waves of discourse on various social media sites, particularly Tumblr. "The discourse" is, at its core, cyberbullying and has had long-term negative effects on ace and aro community spaces and people.

Sometimes "the discourse" focuses on gray or other microlabels, suggesting that "regular" or "real" ace and aro individuals are queer but others who occasionally feel attraction are in some way corrupting the queer community.

Community Involvement

As we will explore in Chapter 7, being involved in aro and ace communities is usually a fundamental aspect of developing and embracing one's orientation. These communities exist around the world and online, and range from intense exploration of identity to conversations about which video-game characters are most likely to be ace or aro. Below are some of the most common ways that aro and ace individuals engage with each other.

GENERAL BLOGGING

Most aro and ace community interactions occur online, often on social media platforms or blogs. Many people have blogs or profiles in which they can discuss how their orientations impact their own lives, talk about community issues, look at the way the world treats their orientation, or even just integrate asexuality and aromanticism into their other interests. These blogs do not exist in a vacuum; many ace and aro bloggers interact with each other in a variety of ways, including, but not limited to, having conversations about different problems they face or their experiences with their identities. These interactions help people new to their identities or new to the communities to understand the nuances of different orientations. There are also events set up to focus community blogging on specific ideas.

BLOGGING CARNIVALS

A Blogging Carnival is a regular event that focuses on a specific topic or theme, where many different bloggers contribute their own blog posts. The carnival's host collects and shares links to the many blog posts, often with their own short commentary on what each blog post contains.

The Carnival of Aces is a monthly event that was started by Sciatrix in 2011 and was inherited by Siggy of The Asexual Agenda Wordpress blog, who still manages it at the time of writing this book. It has covered topics including "Coming Out," "Online Dating," and "Questioning Your Faith." The Carnival of Aros is a newer carnival that was started in 2019, is also monthly, and is managed by the Carnival of Aros Wordpress blog. It has included topics such as "Relationship Anarchy," "Commitment," and "Music." Both carnivals are hosted by a different blog every month.

These Carnivals are an excellent opportunity to get involved with aro and ace communities, as they offer a variety of different experiences on different topics and give newcomers a chance to both make their voices heard through submission of their own work and learn from other community members' submissions. They also allow anyone to suggest a topic for the month, host a carnival, and jump into direct engagement with aro or ace blogging communities.

OTHER PROMPT-BASED INVOLVEMENT

There have been other ace and aro community events organized to encourage blogging and posting on social media via prompts. Often these take the form of one enthusiastic individual composing a list of prompts that many others in the ace or aro communities then use as a jumping-off point for their own content creation, be that writing, vlogging, artwork, poetry, etc. Other times it can be a "challenge" or series of actions one could take, like reading a certain number of books containing canon asexual or aromantic characters. Some of the most popular times for these events to occur are during ASAW in mid-February or Ace Week at the end of October. However, there have been prompt-based events at other times, such as the Asexy April Fanwork Challenges from 2012 through 2015 and Aggressively Arospec Week (June 2021), among others.

There are still other people and groups who provide prompts year-round for writing, art, and community discussions, such as the TAAAP Pride Chats,[11] our own monthly discussion forum on Discord.

GETTING INVOLVED WITH LARGER LGBTQIA+ ORGANIZATIONS

A significant number of LGBTQIA+ organizations do not focus on the needs of less visible orientations and often overlook asexuality and aromanticism entirely. This is changing slowly, with the concerted efforts of aro and ace activists as well as their allies, but there is still a long way to go. Most LGBTQIA+ organizations and coalitions would benefit from ace and aro members telling them that they exist and their issues matter too. This is particularly important when these organizations are planning events or conferences, such as Creating Change or the Human Rights Conference. Many of these organizations also conduct studies of the issues affecting LGBTQIA+ identities, and without ace or aro staffers or volunteers, their identities, experiences, and insight may not be sought out, collected, or reported.

STARTING OR JOINING SOCIAL GROUPS

There are a fair number of social groups for aro and ace people, though they are usually located in metropolitan areas or

---

11   For more information on the TAAAP Pride Chats, see the Appendix.

near college campuses, as well as usually in North America and Europe. Most social groups are specifically asexual or potentially for ace and aro individuals; not many specifically aromantic groups exist. If you want to meet other aro or ace people offline, you can look for a group in your specific area;[12] if one already exists there, you can participate by hosting or attending meetings or gatherings. These gatherings, often organized through the social networking platform meetup.com, can consist of many kinds of activities, including book clubs, bowling, seeing a movie, cookouts, hiking, or simply going out to dinner. If there isn't already a social group, a great way to build up the ace and aro community in the area is to create one, potentially through a larger LGBTQIA+ social group.

PRIDE AND COMMUNITY EVENTS

Showing up to large LGBTQIA+ gatherings to represent asexuality and aromanticism can help integrate aro and ace spectrum identities into the rest of your life. Going to Pride, especially as part of a group, or to a conference, or even a casual social event, can be incredibly self-affirming. Spectators at Pride parades and passersby at Pride festivals might be confused by what asexuality and aromanticism are, but others who are aware of the orientations are typically happy in an impersonal way to see that aces and aros are out and part of the community. On occasions where the person in the crowd is on the ace or aro spectrum themselves, they typically react to seeing aro or ace pride being displayed in a deeply joyful, personal way.

It is essential for other LGBTQIA+ people and allies to see ace and aro people in these celebrations and gatherings, so that they are reminded that we exist. Also, any aro or ace people who feel alone or disconnected from the queer community should

---

12 An extensive list of these in-person social groups can be found at https://acesandaros.org/groups.

be reassured that they do belong, and people might learn about the orientations or discover that there are ace and aro communities locally. Some people might even discover that they belong within these communities!

CHAPTER 3

Our Identity Development Model

Embracing an Ace or Aro Identity

Every ace and aro person has a different story of how they came to accept their identity. For some, things go smoothly. Perhaps they hear the word "aromantic" and immediately realize that it describes their experiences, so they tell everyone they know, who unwaveringly accepts them for who they are. For most, however, the experience is more complicated and challenging. They may experience confusion resulting from a sense of brokenness or difference, and many ace and aro people find it takes a lot of effort and time to fully accept their identities. While each journey is different, there are numerous similarities. We will explore these similarities through an identity development model.

Identity development models are frameworks that are used to outline the typical process of realizing and accepting one's identity. In general, identity development models can be useful for helping you understand your own identity and the way it was formed. They can give you context to help you understand the challenges you may be facing or the joys you are experiencing. The process of discovery and identity formation does not occur on a fixed timeline or in exactly the same way for everyone. No matter where you are in your own journey right now, you should not feel pressure to be at a different part of the process before you are ready; your identity is whatever you define it to be.

One such model is William Cross's five-stage model of Nigrescence, or Black Identity Development, which describes the process African Americans undergo to "become Black" through understanding and embracing their identity;[1] another is the Cass Identity Model, which outlines how gay and lesbian people go through a similar process.[2] Nicole Robbins, Katherine Graff Low, and Anna Query proposed an Asexual Identity Development Model[3] to try to explain the unique ways ace people go through the process of integrating their ace identity into their whole sense of self.

The Asexual Identity Development Model was proposed relatively recently, and not much additional research has been put into analyzing the development of identity in ace people. As far as we know, there has been no research done on identity development in aro people outside of a potential overlapping ace identity. We will be loosely using the Asexual Identity Development Model to organize the rest of this book because we found it to be an efficient way of categorizing the experiences of many different aro and ace people to highlight the common threads among these experiences.

This model is not perfect. It does not deal much with the relationship between aro and ace identity and society. Other identity development models typically synthesize internal

1   Cross, W. E., Jr. (1995) "The Psychology of Nigrescence: Revising the Cross Model." In J. G. Ponterotto, J. M. Casas, L. A. Suzuki, and C. M. Alexander (eds.) *Handbook of Multicultural Counseling* (pp.93–122). Thousand Oaks, CA: Sage Publications, Inc.

2   Cass, V. (1979) "Homosexual identity formation: A theoretical model." *Journal of Homosexuality 4*, 3, 219–235.

3   Robbins, N. K., Low, K. G. and Query, A. N. (2016) "A Qualitative Exploration of the 'Coming Out' Process for Asexual Individuals." *Archives of Sexual Behavior 45*, 751–760.

development with how society determines and characterizes that identity, and this aspect of development is important to consider. While the chapter is organized according to the model as proposed by Robbins *et al.*, we have expanded some stages and added others. Additionally, while we will not be discussing other identity development models in this chapter, other orientation models can provide further understanding.

It is also important to remember that this model was not created in a way that was intended to cover aromanticism as an independent identity, and it downplays the development of an aro identity in those who are both ace and aro. However, due to the similarities we have seen in the development process of an ace identity and an aro identity, we have chosen to use this model to discuss aro experiences as well.

In the following section, we will briefly outline our interpretation of Robbins *et al.*'s model. It is important to note that this model is not linear or universal. Some parts may happen simultaneously or out of order, and some (or all) parts might not apply to a particular person's experience. It is simply a tool to begin to understand the development of aro and ace identity.

Part One: Ignorance

In this part of the process, individuals lack a conceptual knowledge of asexuality or aromanticism and feel a sense of difference and confusion regarding their orientation. This is often expressed as pathologizing one's own lack of sexual or romantic feelings. Some ace and aro people describe this experience as feeling "broken" or feeling like they are the only person who has this experience, and others might be convinced that sexual or romantic attraction isn't real or is an exaggerated experience.

Part Two: Discovery of Terminology

In this part of the process, individuals discover asexuality and aromanticism, as well as the surrounding terminology that they can use to describe their experiences. Compared to some other LGBTQIA+ identities, aro and ace people are more likely to lack the concepts and vocabulary necessary to describe their identities, and it is more difficult to find the information even when looking. This stage may be initiated by the individual searching the internet to try to figure out why their experiences with romantic or sexual attraction differ from their allo peers'. Alternatively, they may come across information about aromanticism and asexuality accidentally, without intentionally seeking answers. Finally, care providers or allies may introduce the information to them.

Please note that Part Two is often not a single event of discovering the terminology, but rather a process of repeatedly discovering the words with greater and greater understanding until one is at a point where they can draw the connection between their own experience and the labels.

Part Three: Identity Confusion

In this part of the process, individuals are aware of aro and ace identities generally, but do not necessarily apply the label to their own experiences. During this part, an ace or aro person may be dealing with many different roadblocks preventing them from accepting or understanding their identity.

Part Four: Exploration and Education

In Part Four, the individual starts participating in various forms of ace or aro communities. Many aro and ace people learn about asexuality or aromanticism through reading and listening to others' experiences online, while some people find those communities in person as well. Robbins *et al.* suggest that this part of the process likely takes place earlier and is more crucial to identity development for ace people than for gay, lesbian, and bisexual people, and we believe that this holds true for aro people as well.

Part Five: Identity Acceptance and Salience Negotiation

Part Five begins when an individual has accepted that their identity is a valid orientation and they no longer feel that they are "broken." Internalized shame and pathologization may linger during this part of the process, but they are now experienced alongside acceptance or are less prominent. In this part, the aro or ace person may begin to better understand their own orientation and explore their identity in more depth. In addition, they will start to think about how being ace or aro will affect the rest of their life and decide the importance of their aro or ace identity to their identity as a whole.

Unlike most LGBTQIA+ identity models, the Asexual Identity Development Model does not include a specific part for Identity Pride, the point at which the individual is fully submersed in their identity and culture, and most of their viewpoints and opinions are colored by their orientation. However, we believe that this point occurs for many aro and ace people as well during this part of the identity development process.

Part Six: Coming Out

This part of the process centers on an aro or ace person's decision to come out. However, coming out as ace or aro is a very different experience than coming out as lesbian, gay, or bisexual, because asexuality and aromanticism are still relatively unknown and misunderstood identities. People may not be receptive to or may doubt the validity of ace and aro identities, so coming out may also require such identities to be defended. How important one's orientation is to their identity as a whole often impacts the decision to come out. For some, this part may not be important or even necessary.

Part Seven: Identity Integration

At this part of the process, an individual accepts their orientation, and they are no longer trying to hide it or conform to their society's expectations regarding sexuality and romance. People in this part may continue to explore the nuances of their identity or even help construct the broader social understanding of ace and aro identities. Their orientation is seamlessly integrated as a part of their overall identity.

However, just reaching identity integration does not mean that the aro or ace person has finished developing their identity, as there are many factors that can impact the way they think of themselves and their orientations. This process is not linear, and there is not necessarily an endpoint.

CHAPTER 4

Part One—Ignorance

Total Lack of Awareness

"It's hard to notice that something is gone when you didn't even know that it existed in the first place."—Alyssa

One of the most difficult parts of someone realizing they have an aro or ace identity is simply knowing the identities are possibilities in the first place. It is next to impossible to even explain patterns of attraction, as usually all an ace or aro person can do is describe the lack of feelings or make comparisons to feelings that others experience. Straight, gay, lesbian, and bi people can point to those they are attracted to and claim their identity based on sexual or romantic attraction. Many aro and ace people cannot do this in the same way. When they are unaware that ace and aro identities exist, aro and ace people usually feel one of three main ways.

- They can assume that it is typical to not experience romantic or sexual attraction, or not experience attraction yet.
- They can assume that they feel the same as their allosexual and alloromantic peers because they are confusing types of attraction (e.g. confusing aesthetic attraction with romantic attraction).

- They know they are different but are unable to parse out exactly how.

It is therefore almost impossible to conceptualize your identity before you recognize the differences or have the vocabulary to do so. Unfortunately, for various reasons, aro and ace people may have little access to vocabulary or general information about aromanticism and asexuality, and many ace and aro people are not able to understand their identity until comparatively late in life as a result.

One factor that contributes to the general lack of awareness of asexuality and aromanticism is media representation.[1] Ace and aro people have very few mainstream examples to which they can compare themselves. Until very recently, there was no media representation of these identities, and the representation that does exist is often inaccurate or unrepresentative. Moreover, because these identities are so unknown, most ace and aro people do not meet other aro or ace people until they seek them out.

Another challenge related to vocabulary is that many orientations can be placed on the ace and aro spectrums. For those who experience attraction rarely or in varying degrees, ace and aro might feel like relevant identities. However, it can be hard to reconcile these identities—which are often framed as a complete lack of attraction—with the few (or mild, or questionable) instances of attraction that one does experience, especially for people who identify as gray or demi. This also runs alongside the reality that many people experience the same orientation in different ways.[2]

Additionally, not knowing the basic framework of attraction can make it hard to parse out one's identity. In mainstream

---

1 See "Aro and Ace Representation in Media" in Chapter 2.
2 See "Asexuality and Aromanticism as Complex Identities" in Chapter 1.

culture, the Kinsey Scale is the most widely known model of attraction, but it does not explicitly account for aro or ace identities;[3] outside of the communities themselves, there is little awareness of models of attraction that do include ace and aro people. Without this framework, aro and ace people might not have the tools they need to explore their identities fully.

> *"If you're getting your vision tested and the ophthalmologist tells you your eyesight is -4.25 in both eyes, then you're near-sighted—and that is a proven fact, with scientific backing, all that. If you are a man and find yourself desiring a man, then you are either gay or bisexual and that is also a socially proven fact. We don't have that kind of gauge with asexuality. And if we do, who's the expert who can check for us? Do we even have one to begin with?"—Macy*

This ignorance of both the vocabulary and the basic framework of attraction impacts aro and ace people in many ways, including before they even begin to understand their identities. For many other orientations and identities, the types of confusion we will describe in this section are more typical of pre-pubescent or early adolescent youth than adults. However, due to this ignorance, it is very common for ace and aro people to experience these feelings well into adulthood.

> *"I think the questioning process is different for asexuals because there is significantly less information about it. If you ask someone when they realized they were gay, they'll say, 'When I was five and had a crush on another little girl.' If you ask someone when they realized they were ace, they'll say, 'When I finally heard the word asexual for the first time.' It can also be hard because you have to detect the lack of something.*

---

3   See "Models of Attraction and Orientation" in Chapter 1.

> *This requires aces to compare their sexual 'progress' with their peers and recognize that something is 'missing.'"—Becca*

Impact of Lack of Awareness

Before aro and ace people realize they are aro or ace, they often experience some sense of being different from their peers. They may know that it's their approach to sexual or romantic topics that makes them different, or they may just know that they have difficulty relating to others without being able to pinpoint exactly why.

Ace and aro people might not notice that they're different from their peers right away. For some, this may be a sudden realization that occurs when somebody says something utterly baffling to the ace or aro person. For others, it may happen more gradually, with many scenarios building up until this sense of difference rises to the level of conscious thought. They might even discover this difference when someone says something entirely relatable and they realize it is the first time someone has discussed romance or sex in a way that makes sense.

This sense of difference can make many people in this part feel broken. Some people might not be bothered by this difference, or even fully notice it, until external forces convince them that they are broken. Ace people might seek medical help to get their hormones checked, and aro people might think they have some sort of fear of intimacy or commitment. Both aro and ace people might try to force themselves into relationships and situations that they are uncomfortable with in order to try to "fix" themselves.

> *"I can say with certainty now, though, that what isolation and confusion I felt for all of my teen years and part of my twenties would have been eliminated entirely had I heard about the concept of asexuality when I was younger."—Anonymous*

Aro and ace people might be confused by others' behaviors. They might not understand why their peers are so interested in sex or romantic relationships. It's a common misconception among young ace and aro people that their peers might be faking or exaggerating their sexual or romantic attraction and interests. Strange as it may seem, many aro and ace people think that the entire concept of finding someone attractive or having a crush is entirely fake.

Aro and ace people might also come up with explanations for their lack of or different kind of attraction, including, but not limited to, the following.

- They just haven't gotten to this point yet: they are a "late bloomer" and will at some point feel the same kind of sexual or romantic attraction that they see from their peers.
- Their specific personality traits, such as social anxiety, introversion, or repression, prevent them from feeling attraction.
- They believe (or have internalized) generalizations about another one of their identities, such as religion, race, gender, neurodiversity, or disability.[4]
- They may believe that they are above the petty dramas caused by romantic and sexual desires they see around them.[5]
- They believe that their personal experiences, which may include trauma of some kind, preclude attraction.

"With my high-school theories debunked, I started to believe my lack of attraction was something I had to fix. Maybe I

---

4   See "Influences of Other Identities" in Chapter 6.
5   Many ace and aro people continue believing this after this part, and it may turn into sex- or romance-negativity. For more, see "Negativity Towards Romance or Sex" in Chapter 8.

was repressed due to my conservative religion. Maybe I was afraid of intimacy. Maybe I was childish or too picky. Maybe I just had to work harder at becoming attracted to someone. These thoughts didn't cause a great amount of distress, but I was concerned at times. Although I didn't want a partner at the time, I worried that I would miss my chance to find a good partner while I was working through how to be 'properly attracted' to people."—Anonymous

Attraction Confusion

One of the other common experiences is not realizing the difference or lack of attraction due to confusing some kinds of attraction for others and assuming that the attraction being felt is the romantic and/or sexual attraction discussed by peers.

Most people have difficulty distinguishing between romantic, sexual, aesthetic, sensual, and other forms of attraction. This means that it can be hard for aro and ace people to realize that either they don't feel one of those forms of attraction or they feel it in a significantly different way than allo people. Many people who are both alloromantic and allosexual discuss their experiences in a way that conflates most attractions, especially romantic and sexual, and the differences between the types of attraction may not be immediately apparent. Ace and aro people may believe that if they feel one part of the overall experience described by both allo people and by society at large, they feel all forms of attraction.

This confusion intensifies when other forms of attraction are brought into play. In one hypothetical, an aroace person who doesn't realize their identities yet might meet someone and click with them, want to be physically and emotionally close, and admire how they look. That person is experiencing a squish, as well as sensual and aesthetic attraction, but describing it without the words "squish," "sensual," or "aesthetic" might give the impression that they are romantically and sexually attracted. All of these attractions can be mixed and felt differently, giving varying impressions of romantic or sexual attraction.

Any and all attractions can be felt infrequently, or less strongly than is considered typical. In other cases, a form of attraction can be felt in a way that is hard to differentiate from other attractions. Therefore, graysexual and grayromantic people might not understand why they feel attraction with different clarity, intensity, or frequency, while allo people around them fall in love or lust so certainly, intensely, or quickly.

> *"The only obstacle I faced was that I felt weird in that I still enjoyed some kinds of touch—kissing and cuddling for example. But the more I read, the more I understood that asexuality is a spectrum, which made me comfortable in accepting the unique combination of feelings that is me."—Anonymous*

Often there are at least some experiences and desires that ace or aro people have which allo people also have, so many ace and aro people don't initially doubt their "normalcy." They may spend years focusing on the similarities while repressing or denying the feelings and experiences that don't align with the experiences of people who are both alloromantic and allosexual.

> *"However, with every orientation, you have those that know from the start and those that must enter a rollercoaster of ups and downs before they can secure themselves at the station. Am I just asexual, or gray-asexual? Do I desire some sexual connection, or am I repulsed by the idea of any contact at all? Am I happy on my own, or do I prefer some type of partner in my life? Unless you meet someone willing to help you explore, there's hardly a way for asexuals and aromantics to mess around without feeling like we are stepping people on their toes or fooling them somehow. People question us as much as*

*we question ourselves, which makes exploring our needs freely
limited and exhausting."—Sara S*

Yet little tells may appear that resonate differently for ace and
aro people in a way that shows them the attraction they feel is
different from the attractions their peers describe. Friends or
acquaintances might mention feelings that don't quite resonate
with the ace or aro person. For example, friends will express
sexual attraction to others over and over and in detail, in ways
that seem unrealistic or inaccurate to an ace person. On the
other hand, an aro person may hear friends and acquaintances
describe desires or pleasure in relation to romantic acts or relationships that they are indifferent to or repulsed by.

Trying to Fit In

Either because they think others are faking their attraction
or because they are trying to fit in with their peers, ace and
aro people might find themselves faking romantic and sexual
attraction. While aro and ace communities might typically
define crushes as an experience relating to romantic attraction,
in broader society, they are often used to express both sexual
and romantic attraction. As a result, ace people who are not aro
might find themselves faking crushes due to not experiencing
sexual attraction.

Alternatively, due to confusion over kinds of attraction,
some aro or ace people might claim a crush based on non-
romantic or non-sexual attraction or based on only one of those
attractions or a different kind of attraction altogether. Here are
some examples:

- Binti, who is alloaro, may think that she has a crush
  on Jaeho because of her sexual attraction, not realizing
  that she doesn't feel romantic attraction.

- George, who is alloace, may think he has a crush on Ahmed based solely on his romantic feelings, but not feel attracted to him sexually at all.
- Diya, who is aroace, may think she has a crush on Na'estse based on her aesthetic attraction, but she really just wants to look at her.

> *"I used to fake a crush on one of my best friends, just because I thought that was what I was supposed to do. Looking back though I knew it felt wrong and was afraid of driving him away."*—Heather

Ace and aro people often engage in certain behaviors or enter into certain types of relationships because they feel they should. There are many sexual and romantic behaviors and experiences that society treats as normative. Most people consider these experiences to be rites of passage, and thus they are considered necessary experiences for all people.

Therefore, ace people sometimes choose to engage in sexual activities for reasons other than sexual attraction or sex-favorability. Let's consider Fatima, an ace person. Fatima might have sex for a variety of complex factors, particularly if they do not know that they are ace yet.

- Fatima may think that they are too old to be a virgin and that they are not a proper adult without having that experience.
- As a teen, they may have internalized that everyone eventually experiences sexual attraction, and they may think that they must already experience sexual attraction without recognizing it or that it will soon happen.
- They might believe that sex is an extremely enjoyable experience and they are deprived of that pleasure without sex.

- They might believe that they will feel sexual attraction and relate more to their allosexual peers once they have sex.
- They might believe they need to have sex in a specific way or with a specific person to feel sexual attraction.
- Fatima might be in a romantic relationship, and they may not believe that it is possible to be romantic without sexual activity or may feel that they cannot deny their partner forever.
- They may also assume that the sensual attraction that they are experiencing is sexual.

Fatima does not have to be actively coerced or pressured for any of the above reasons to hold true. Ace people sometimes have more difficulty understanding their desire or lack thereof because many societies have taboos around discussing sex, sexual behavior, or sexual attraction in an open or frank way. This ignorance around sex as a whole contributes to ace people's specific ignorance around their own attractions.[6]

Similarly, aro people sometimes choose to engage in romantic behaviors for reasons other than romantic attraction or romance-favorability. Many societies have a very strong amatonormative bent, telling everyone that romantic love is the most important kind of relationship and that life without romance is meaningless. Conversely, the fear of ending up alone is pervasive and expected, typically discussed quite narrowly in the sense of living an entire life without finding a romantic partner to marry, with no consideration that one could be content in a more solitary life or could find company in non-romantic relationships of various kinds.

For example, Draco is an aro person. They might take part in romantic behaviors for many reasons, especially if they don't know that they are aro.

---

6   For more, see "Compulsory Sexuality" in Chapter 6.

- Draco may think they cannot be happy without finding a long-term romantic companion or without the experience of falling in love.
- As a child, they may have internalized the narrative that they will eventually grow up, get married, and live happily ever after.
- Draco may think that engaging in romantic behaviors and relationships will help them develop romantic attractions.
- Draco may feel guilty for having sexual attraction or engaging in sexual behavior outside of a romantic relationship or may feel that it is necessary to be romantic to have sex.
- Draco might have thought the alterous attraction they felt was romantic.
- They may have dated because of peer pressure and shame.
- They may not have wanted to hurt the feelings of someone who asked them out.

The lack of importance placed on respecting others' romantic boundaries can compound these experiences. Consent is rarely emphasized outside of a sexual context. Because so many societies place romance on a high pedestal, it may be hard for aro people to understand their own boundaries and comfort levels.[7]

Are There Turtles in the Pond?
There is a well-known Tumblr post from pinkdiamondprince[8] that summarizes the overall frustration of being ace or aro and

---

7   For more on amatonormativity, see "Amatonormativity" in Chapter 6.
8   Pinkdiamondprince (2016) "This Be My Blog." Accessed on 24/5/2022 at https://pinkdiamondprince.tumblr.com/post/154254157173/trying-to-figure-out-if-youre-ace-or-aro-can-be.

not knowing or understanding that yet, and trying to find or understand attraction. In this metaphor, the turtles are attraction, whether sexual, romantic, or both. The post begins:

> Trying to figure out if you're ace or aro can be so goddamn hard because it's like, trying to find the absence of something. Imagine you're at a pond and you want to know if there are any turtles, or fish. Say you find a turtle and you're like "great! Now I know there are turtles." [...]
>
> But like, if you don't find any turtles it might be that there are no turtles or maybe you're just really shitty at looking for turtles and maybe you THINK you saw a turtle over there or maybe it was just a stick. Maybe there are only a few turtles. Maybe you need to do something special to find the turtles. Maybe a bunch of these rocks are actually turtles but you couldn't tell them apart. Maybe there are no turtles. You have no idea.

Overall, the metaphor is apt. It is impossible to "prove a negative," and being aro or ace means having no or limited attraction in some way. You can only start to look for turtles once you know that turtles exist.

> *"I think questioning for aces is different from other LGBTQ identities because we have to question an absence or a perceived lack of something. If everybody seems to have something that you don't, how can you explain it?"—Steph B*

CHAPTER 5

Part Two—Discovery of Terminology

Modern ace and aro communities only began emerging and offering spaces for people to discuss their experiences in the early 2000s. As a result, many aro and ace people haven't had the conceptual frameworks necessary to understand their experiences and have experienced these feelings of confusion and difference well into adulthood. This is especially true for older aces and aros. Ace and aro people in specific cultures and with specific identities may face stronger barriers to discovering or accepting these frameworks—for example, there are many parts of the world that make it difficult to access any LGBTQIA+ affirming information, which would also limit access to information about aromanticism and asexuality. In addition, most of the resources that exist are not accessible to people with various disabilities (cognitive, physical, and emotional) or people who do not speak English. These resources tend to assume that their readers are living in English-speaking, Western societies. Even beyond that, getting information to people with limited internet access and in parts of the world that don't affirm LGBTQIA+ identities has not been a priority in aro or ace communities.

> *"[W]e had to volunteer at a resource center for LGBTQ youth. I loved it so much that I wanted to come back as a real volunteer*

> *after I graduated. And so I did. During the volunteer orien-*
> *tation, we were given packets (more extensive than when I*
> *volunteered as a student), with brief descriptions of various*
> *orientations and gender identities. One of these was asexual-*
> *ity. And it was like a light went off, and a huge weight lifted off*
> *my shoulders. Sounds cheesy, but it's true. I went home and did*
> *research on asexuality, and realized this was me."—Kendra*

Discovery of terminology is significant enough to constitute an entire part of the process of identity development for ace and aro people due to the societal ignorance around aromanticism and asexuality. Most sexual identity development models, such as Cass's and Fassinger's models of gay and lesbian identity development, rely on the assumption that their subjects would know that gay and lesbian identities exist. We cannot assume that people will know about asexuality and aromanticism.

Ace and aro people rarely discover the terms for their identity at school, through popular media, or while interacting with others. This is changing, however, and as visibility and awareness improve, more people are starting to learn about asexuality and aromanticism in their childhood or adolescence.

People find out about asexuality and aromanticism in many ways. They might look for information on LGBTQIA+ identities, or they might stumble across the words and look to find out more about the communities. However, in order to actively look for a label without knowing that it exists, a person must already be self-aware enough to know that other labels do not fit them and that they are unlike most other people. This is particularly difficult given how descriptions of sexual and romantic attraction vary from person to person.

Currently, most aro and ace people discover asexuality and aromanticism through the internet. In the 2019 Ace Community Survey, about one fifth of respondents found out about asexuality from Tumblr, and another 30 percent found out through other internet forums, including YouTube, AVEN, Wikipedia, and even Pinterest.[1]

> *"The first time I ever heard the word asexual was on Tumblr. Tumblr gets a lot of bad rep for being obsessed with queer-related topics, but it is also a way to spread information. I would not have found out about asexuality if it weren't for Tumblr. I don't remember the post exactly, but the description fit me almost exactly."*—JLTodd

There is no aro equivalent to this survey, but anecdotally, many aro people discover their identity through the ace community.

> *"I started questioning whether I was aro or alloro during my first year of grad school. I had been active in online ace communities for a few months, and a lot of the aces I was following were also on the aromantic spectrum. I had found myself identifying more with them than with the alloro aces, and that confused me."*—Rebecca C

For many ace and aro people, Part Two is a process of repeatedly discovering the terms and learning about them in more depth until they can connect the words to their own experiences. You may feel a connection to these terms immediately, or you may feel a connection after encountering the terms again and again. The length of time or the number of exposures it takes for you to make these connections does not mean that you are "more" or "less" aro or ace.

---

1   Weis, R., Hermann, L., Bauer, C., Miller, T. L., *et al.* (2021) *The 2019 asexual Community Survey Summary Report*. The Ace Community Survey Team. Accessed on 4/5/2022 at https://asexualcensus.wordpress.com/2019-asexual-community-survey-summary-report.

Reactions to Discovering the Terms

There are many ways that aro and ace people react to hearing the terms "aromantic" and "asexual" for the first time, but they generally fall into a few distinct categories. Because of factors including societal norms, the variety of microlabels, and the experience of coming across a term for the first time, reactions to single specific terms can vary within the aro and ace communities. For example, there are different stigmas around being aromantic and being asexual, and those societal norms impact aces and aros differently. These reactions can apply not just to the broad terms "aromantic" or "asexual," but also to discovering any specific vocabulary within the ace and aro communities. People may discover a microlabel that fits them perfectly or a term that encapsulates an experience they have had.

Relief at Finding a Fitting Label and/or Community

As explained in Chapter 4, many ace and aro people feel broken after they realize the differences that exist between themselves and others. Finding the label of "asexual" or "aromantic" means having a word and identity that helps encompass and express their experiences. Additionally, discovering the terms often also includes finding a community of people who can validate their experiences. Being able to finally relate to others' experiences can be exciting, refreshing, or comforting. However, that relief may not be the sole response. Some people might be relieved but still confused, because the identity they've learned about doesn't quite match up with their experiences as someone in the gray area of the aromantic or asexual spectrums.

> *"Discovering I was aroace was, I think, the happiest part of my life. I feel like before my discovery, I was only half the person I could be, always hiding away a part of myself, never knowing my full potential as a human being. After my discovery, the immense feeling of freedom it gave me cannot be adequately*

described. Everything that ever happened in my life suddenly clicked into place and everything made sense. I finally understood who I was and what I wanted out of life, and I finally understood that there was nothing wrong with me."—TB

Fully Realizing Otherness

On the other hand, also as described in Chapter 4, some aro and ace people have never thought of themselves as different from anyone else. When they discover the asexual and aromantic orientations, these ace and aro people might be jarred by the realization that their experiences with attraction are atypical. This can also be very difficult to accept—ace and aro people may begin thinking that they are broken, since almost nobody they know has had similar experiences. With this realization, the person might experience disappointment that there will always be a gap in understanding and in experience between them and allo people.

"[I]n my mind, I honestly thought it was a big charade that everyone was in on. Like, you have to say you like sex even though no one really does. Little did I know that my friends probably were genuinely enjoying their experiences because they are allosexual. It wasn't until many years after this that I came to realize how my asexuality made my experiences different."—Miranda B

Rejection of the Terminology

The third distinct category of reaction is the rejection of the identities, either in totality or as they apply to themselves. If someone accepts that they are aro or ace, then they will probably need to rethink their worldview, their personal history, and their imagined future. Perhaps subconsciously, some people may instead decide to avoid this self-examination, and the feelings that come with it, in the form of denial, disbelief, and incomprehension.

Many of the respondents we talked to described coming to the realization that their aro or ace identity meant that they did not fit within societal norms and did not relate to how the majority of other people approach romantic or sexual relationships. If you have always assumed you experience fairly average feelings when it comes to sexual or romantic attraction, it could be profoundly uncomfortable to begin to realize how different from the norm you actually are when you learn about the concepts of asexuality or aromanticism. This discomfort causes some aro or ace people to reject the labels and identities.

> "By the time I was 17 or 18 I was aware that asexuality existed. Once in a while I thought in passing 'Maybe I'm asexual,' but I would always push the idea away. I think I had some internalized homophobia and thought that anyone in the LGBTQ community was somehow abnormal or fundamentally different. And I was a pretty normal person, so how could I be a part of it?"—Anonymous

Some people who initially feel this way later describe themselves as having been in denial. At first, they might vehemently reject the labels and identities by distancing themselves from ace or aro communities and any people who associate with them. Some people may also engage in a variety of behaviors, perhaps attempting to prove—to themselves or to others—that they are not aro or ace. They may, in order to overcompensate, engage in acts such as dating someone, kissing, having sex, or exaggerating their romantic or sexual experiences.

These three types of reactions are not mutually exclusive. Many people feel two of these reactions or all three, either simultaneously or recursively. Feeling multiple reactions that may conflict with each other can create even more confusion.

"I was alternating between being glad I had a word to describe my identity and feeling broken."—Maude

OUR ADVICE

- Allow yourself to feel any kind of reaction to discovering you may be aro or ace—this can be a significant change and you can feel however you want about it.
- Read other ace and aro people's stories in blogs, YouTube videos, or any of the other community resources in the Appendix—you may find comfort and guidance in their journeys.
- If English is not your primary language or a language you feel comfortable using, look for the terms that are used in your language or culture.
- Know that it may take time to fully process your reaction.
- Consider discussing your reaction with someone you trust. However, it is important to make sure that the person will validate you and not reject or dismiss you.[2]
- Don't feel compelled to continue exploring. It is okay to take a break for as long as you need and return only when you feel ready to do so. It is also okay to stop exploring if you do not feel that learning more is useful to you.

Bringing Up the Possibility

If you are reading this book because you think you might be ace, aro, or both, you have probably had experiences that align with these identities.

---

2   See Chapter 9, "Part Six—Coming Out," for more about the possible negative reactions that many ace and aro people may experience.

However, even if you are not aro or ace, you can be an ally to others in your life by learning about these identities and the experiences that many of us have. People often learn about aromanticism and asexuality from people they know. For instance, 15.7 percent of respondents from the 2019 Ace Community Survey discovered asexuality through word of mouth, and another 3.6 percent found asexuality through the LGBTQIA+ community (excluding Tumblr). Through reading this book, you have the power to help other people who might be ace or aro but do not know yet that the concepts of asexuality and aromanticism exist.

Many ace and aro people express some or all of the following experiences:

- not knowing what their sexual orientation is
- not feeling like they have had many, if any, crushes in their life
- feeling like all the crushes they have had are not like other people's crushes
- not liking sex
- not wanting any romantic relationship
- knowing they never want to get married
- feelings of repulsion or aversion towards sex, romance, or both
- feeling like they know their orientation, but are "bad" at it or "broken"
- considering themselves a late bloomer who has not yet experienced the feelings others their age have
- feeling like they have experienced these feelings but that they were not as distinct or intense as the way other people describe them
- only very rarely feeling sexual or romantic attractions or desires, or only after a strong emotional connection

- having not yet met the "right person" with whom they could imagine a satisfying romantic relationship or sexual encounter
- feeling confused as to why romance and/or sex is considered a priority by their culture or peers
- confusion about why they have not had a fulfilling or exciting experience with sex and/or romance while being unable to pinpoint what was "wrong" about the relationship or partner
- any other experiences discussed in Part One.

If these experiences match your own, you may want to continue exploring asexuality and aromanticism and whether any of these labels apply to you. If these experiences match those of someone you know, you may want to consider asking if the person has heard of the asexual and aromantic spectrums. However, even if you are also ace or aro, this must be done carefully, as it is never appropriate to decide an orientation for someone else. It is best to give the person in question the frameworks with which to discover their identities for themselves.

> *"I confided in my best friend that I was desperate to figure out why I didn't ever want to have sex. She is a wonderful person who simply told me, 'Oh! Maybe you're asexual!' She had read about asexuality and demisexuality before, so she helped me look up the word 'asexual' online, and it was as if the heavens opened up. I wasn't broken! There were people like me!"—Miranda B*

Many people might want to learn more at this point. If you are not interested in or reject these labels, don't pressure yourself to explore more. Similarly, if you introduce these identities to someone else but they are not interested, don't pressure them to talk about aro or ace identities or experiences. It will typically take time for someone to reflect on their experiences before they figure out if any of these identities are applicable. It is important for all potentially aro or ace people to know that there is a community of ace or aro people for them to join and that if they do ultimately feel like they are on the ace or aro spectrums, they won't be alone.

OUR ADVICE TO ALLIES

- Consider sharing some of the resources we list in the Appendix with them to allow them to do their own research.
- Do not presume that any person is definitely ace or aro.
- Do not even imply to them that you believe they "probably" or "most likely" are or are not aro or ace.
- Leave your views on the spectrums and the person's identity neutral. Kindly and calmly make it clear that it is entirely okay whether or not they determine they are ace or aro.
- If you are aro or ace yourself, it is also helpful to share this identity with the other person to physically show that they are not alone.

Getting the Word Out

This book is not the final word on aro and ace identities, and we highly recommend seeking out additional resources to learn more. There is a spectrum of sexual and romantic desires beyond absolute zero sexual or romantic attraction. If you bring this up in conversation, people who you would not have thought would be aro or ace may discover their identity through you or simply learn something about amatonormativity and compulsory sexuality, and make positive changes in their life. Additionally, people you help educate about ace and aro identities may become much-needed supportive allies to ace and aro communities.

There are many spaces that can spread more information about aro and ace identities and experiences to the public. For example:

- LGBTQIA+ centers and organizations, including in schools, universities, and online
- libraries
- student centers at universities
- sex education classes
- therapist's and doctor's offices
- community centers.

If these spaces don't have any aro or ace resources, you can request that they start providing some.[3] Anyone can and should advocate for these resources, provided it is safe to do so, no matter their identity. In general, just rethinking any assumptions that everyone feels the same or similar attractions can be helpful to those who do not.

> *"[After I mentioned asexuality, my cousin] came to me with tears in their eyes, saying they finally understood themselves, and realized they weren't broken. I don't think I've ever again been so touched by someone's coming out, so proud to be aroace, or so glad that I talk so openly about asexuality and aromanticism. Because of one simple statement of mine, this child discovered their sexuality [...]*
>
> *Words have so much power. If I, if we all, keep talking about this, spreading knowledge, normalizing this identity, we can reach so many people, we can stop so much self-hatred and*

---

3   For some examples of these resources, see the Appendix.

ignorance and bigotry. That is something I wish to fight for, and try to turn into reality, a little bit more every day. People tend to focus on the pride parades and the loud, aggressive queers, but this is just as important. It's the little things that matter."—Kai

CHAPTER 6

Part Three—Identity Confusion

Disclaimer

Although we share the best advice we can based on our research and our own experiences, we are not licensed therapists, though many of us have spent countless years in therapy. We encourage you to seek out asexuality- and aromanticism-affirming mental health care if you would like professional support navigating any confusion or distress in your identity development process. Also, while we discuss the additional challenges that multiply marginalized aro and ace people face in one specific section of this chapter, it should be understood that these difficulties extend to every roadblock here. Facing stressors stemming from different marginalizations, including racism, sexism, homophobia, transphobia, classism, and ableism, can make this part of the process more challenging. It is important to give yourself the space, resources, and kindness that you deserve while working through your identity confusion.

We have also collected resources from other aromantic and asexual people discussing many of the experiences described in this chapter, and we encourage you to look through those in the Appendix.

Ace-Specific Experiences
Experiences with Low and Non-Existent Libido

Much of society considers a low sex drive (or the lack of a sex drive altogether) to be a medical symptom that should be cured. As a result, it is possible that ace people without libidos may internalize the idea that they are broken, especially before beginning to identify as ace. They might seek out a sex therapist, change their medications, try drinking alcohol or engaging in recreational drug use to decrease inhibitions, or engage in sexual or masturbatory activities they do not desire innately but feel pressured into by peers, partners, or society. Ace people who are going against their natural lack of desire may suffer from regret or shame, or end up in dangerous or traumatizing situations. For many people who experience distress about a low libido, that distress comes from not being able to meet society's or a partner's expectations rather than truly wanting to experience libido and arousal for themselves.

Low or non-existent libido can manifest in more than one way. Many people experience a change in their libido due to age, medication, mental health, physical health, stress level, relationship status, and other factors. There is a difference between someone's libido lowering and someone who never had a libido in the first place. There are a significant number of ace people who have never had a libido. Someone's perspective on their low or non-existent libido will be affected by multiple factors including if they had a libido at an earlier point in time and if they enjoyed the experience of having a libido.

Many aces without libidos do not feel that increasing their libido, even if it were possible, would be a positive thing. A lack of libido is considered by many ace people to be a natural variance that exists rather than a medical problem that needs to be solved. The distress felt by people with low or non-existent libidos is often connected to societal pressure to engage in sex rather than an innate desire. For many people who have low or non-existent libidos, learning about asexuality and applying that label to themselves is simply giving them the permission to be who they naturally are.

Ace people without libidos may face some difficulties when first engaging with ace communities. In some ace communities, people stress that asexuality has "nothing to do with" lacking a libido and that it is normal for aces to masturbate and have functional reproductive organs. These types of comments are made to combat misconceptions that all ace people are 100 percent non-sexual in every conceivable way, but sometimes the generalizations are stated in such a way that leads those who don't have libidos to feel even more broken or to feel like they don't fit in with the experiences of most other aces.

> *"I feel unnatural for having no libido or not experiencing sexual arousal. There is no medical reason for me to feel this way (believe me, I've been poked and prodded and discounted so many times by the medical community), it's because I'm asexual. I want to disclose it to people so they understand me, but I either get jokes or people asking about my thyroid."*—Anonymous

OUR ADVICE

If you are not distressed by your lack of libido:

- That's great! Don't listen to anyone who tells you that your lack of libido is a medical problem that needs addressing.
- Remember, you don't have to identify as ace if you don't want to, even if you resonate with the experiences here, as not all people who lack a libido identify as ace.
- If you are wondering whether you might be ace,

know that lacking a libido is a legitimate reason many identify as ace.

If you are distressed by your lack of libido:

- You do not need to find a medical cause (e.g. getting your hormones checked).
- Determine the source of your distress, and work on how to insulate yourself from the pressure to be allosexual. Allosexual is not the only way to be!
- It is still valid to explore ways of medically increasing your libido or sexual function, even if you do identify as ace. This should always be your decision, and you should not be pressured into taking that option by anyone, including doctors, therapists, partners, or friends. The focus should be on reducing your distress and increasing your comfort and happiness.

Experiences with Libido and Sexual Activities

A common misconception about asexuality is that a prerequisite for identifying as ace includes a lack of a libido or a complete disinterest in engaging in any kind of sexual activity. A questioning person might feel like they cannot identify as ace because they have a sex drive, masturbate, watch porn, or engage in partnered sex. This isn't true! They absolutely can.

People usually identify as asexual due to the lack of at least one of the following aspects of sexuality: sexual attraction, sexual desire, libido or sex drive, arousal, and sexual behavior, though they may still experience several of these. While outside of ace communities, there is often no large distinction made between those aspects, understanding the differences can be crucial when it comes to accepting an ace identity. There are many ace people who experience little or no sexual attraction but do experience sexual desire and a libido, and potentially also engage in sexual activities. Many people don't realize this when they are first questioning their identity and believe that they can't possibly be ace because they get aroused, watch porn, or engage in some other sexual activity.

> *"[O]nce I discovered [asexuality] I was still confused if I was asexual because of my sexual fetish; however I found because it really had nothing to do with sex, it made it easier to understand what my orientation is."*—Edward

> *"I encountered the word 'asexual' online in my early twenties, but didn't think it applied to me because I enjoyed reading erotic scenes and masturbating. It is only within the past year at age 28 I realized many aces masturbate."*—Minerva

OUR ADVICE

- Learn the differences between sexual attraction, sexual desire, libido/sex drive, arousal, and sexual behaviors, and apply those concepts to your own experiences, if that's useful for you.
- If the distinction between some of these terms is not helpful, feel free to identify with the factors that make the most sense to you. Some people don't find it useful to separate all of these because the lines blur too much, and that's fine!
- Read about other words ace communities use to describe these experiences, such as "aegosexual," "sex-indifferent," "sex-favorable," or "undirected sex drive."
- Know that engaging in sexual behaviors or experiencing a libido does not prevent you from being ace.
- Seek out stories from ace people who do experience

and engage in these aspects of sexuality to help you see that you are not alone in these experiences.

- Consider talking to an affirming friend or therapist about any other negative feelings you may have around your experiences with libido or sexuality.

Compulsory Sexuality

Societal norms create the expectation that an intrinsic part of being human is being sexual, desiring sex, and enjoying having sex. Sex education aimed at adolescents often discusses "when you are ready to have sex," as if feeling "ready" is inevitable. Rarely does sex education present sex as something that people may not ever want. Moreover, "losing one's virginity" is seen as a rite of passage. Consider also the difference between divorce and annulment, where annulment presumes the marriage was not legitimate if it was not consummated (consummated is the legal term for when a couple has sex for the first time after being married). Additionally, remember the political struggle it took for marital rape to be considered possible, as sex is so expected within the context of a marriage. Ridiculing virgins, especially adult virgins, as "losers," "undesirable," and "naive" is common, and many people start to feel a sense of shame over being a virgin after most or all of their peers no longer are.

As the common adage goes, "sex sells"; constant reminders of how most people are allosexual and interested in sex can be found in most forms of entertainment including tabloid articles, popular music, books, TV, films, comic books, video games, advertisements, and more. Common advice on how to make a romantic relationship "healthy" and lasting often states that sex must be had regularly or else something is wrong. Sex can often be described as a life-changing experience, and many things are jokingly compared to sex as if sex is truly the ultimate experience of enjoyment or fulfillment. Any one or more of these factors can lead someone with no intrinsic sexual desire, including some people who are sex-repulsed, to repress any feelings of discomfort they feel regarding the idea of sex.

People may be in denial about their own desires or lack thereof, especially when they have not heard of asexuality and all society has ever told them is that every adult must want sex. These ace people may "want to want" sex and indeed long for the experience of desire, even when no actual sexual attraction or desire is present. This can lead to ace people placing themselves in jeopardizing positions in an attempt to feel that elusive "spark." Ace people can also place the onus on themselves to enjoy sex rather than understanding that compulsory sexuality has negatively impacted them and that it is quite common to have a range of feelings about various sexual activities.

> *"I realize now that even when I was sexually active, I was viewing sex in a very asexual way (i.e. it was another thing to be good at, even though I didn't desire it or find it particularly gratifying)."*—Eris V

OUR ADVICE

- Understand that sex may not be as central to other people as it seems, and there's an exaggerated level of sex-obsession in society.
- Be aware that compulsory sexuality is incredibly pervasive, and it is even more pervasive for certain minoritized groups based on intersecting systems of oppression. Know that while not feeling sexual attraction does not free anyone from this pressure, you do not need to give into it.
- You do not have to feel guilt or frustration with your past selves for engaging in sexual activities.
- You also do not have to feel guilty for wanting sex

if you are sex-favorable; you are not responsible for destroying compulsory sexuality through your actions. Wanting sex does not mean that you perpetuate the idea that *everyone* should want sex.

- Know that there are others out there who don't prioritize sex and that you can pursue a partnership without sex if you want.
- Remember that happiness is not derived from completing a checklist of "fundamental" life experiences, and nobody checks them all off.

Aro-Specific Experiences
What is Romance?

The question "What is romance?" is often asked as a part of questioning and coming to an aromantic spectrum identity. What romance is—and, more specifically, what romantic attraction is—can be hard to pin down for those who do not experience it or who experience it differently than alloromantic people.

Many in the early stages of understanding aromanticism struggle with the idea that action is not attraction—that actions typically seen by society as romantic do not necessarily indicate romantic feelings. Behavior does not necessarily determine whether or not someone is aro. Some aro people may be averse to, or repulsed by, any romantic or romantic-coded actions. Conversely, other aro people may engage in actions that their culture deems romantic, such as hand holding or going on dates, without feeling attracted to the person or people they are engaging in those actions with. Neither of these groups is "more aro" or "less aro" than the other.

In this vein, romance is not seen as fulfilling a set of actions, but rather having a certain feeling. For aro people, this feeling is absent or experienced differently than alloromantic people, whether romantic-coded actions are present or not. This feeling may vary by culture and by individual, but the common thread among aro people is a disconnect from the typical emotional experience associated with romance. This disconnect can be an important factor in identifying as aromantic.

Furthermore, romance is highly subjective. Going out to see a movie, getting dinner, and walking along arm in arm can be seen as romantic or as platonic, depending on the feelings of the individuals involved. This can make it particularly difficult to identify as aro, particularly for romance-neutral or romance-favorable aros who don't necessarily mind or even enjoy stereotypically romantic behaviors.

> *"I think I can view past me as being aro/ace and not fully realizing it, although I have played out crushes and dated a few people down the road—mainly because I think I never fully understood what romance was supposed to be. As a child you tend to be heavily exposed to romantic subplots in movies, TV shows and things you read; and with that you want to be able to relate to the characters and the people around you who are, in their run, expressing needs whether it be romantic or sexual. I was merely mirroring what I thought was the normal thing to be and do, what my friends did and what I got exposed to."—Sarah S*

OUR ADVICE

- Feel free to identify as aromantic if the identity resonates with you for any reason. You do not need to fully define what romance is before you can be sure you're aro.
- Understand that most alloromantic people cannot define romance either.
- Learn the differences between romantic attraction,

romantic desire, platonic attraction, alterous attraction, and other aro community terms that might be relevant, then apply those concepts to your own experiences if and where they fit.

- Seek out stories from aro people to help see that you are not alone in your experiences.
- Explore various aro-spectrum identities, such as "quoiromantic" and "grayromantic," that can be used by those who have uncertain or confusing feelings about what romantic attraction is.

Amatonormativity

Amatonormativity is a term coined by Elizabeth Brake that refers to the disproportionate focus on and prioritization of romantic relationships above all else as well as the widespread assumption that finding romantic love is a universally shared goal. Amatonormativity describes the systemic way in which these sociocultural ideas and norms are upheld—this includes the formal institutionalization of marriage and the thousands of legal benefits it confers.

> This consists in the assumptions that a central, exclusive, amorous relationship is normal for humans, in that it is a universally shared goal, and that such a relationship is normative, in that it should be aimed at in preference to other relationship types.[1]

Amatonormativity impacts both aro people and alloromantic people. Some aro people struggle with distinguishing platonic feelings from romantic ones or feel more confused after being told by others that their platonic feelings must be romantic. Very

---

1   Brake, E. (2012) *Minimizing Marriage: Marriage, Morality, and the Law.* Oxford: Oxford University Press.

often, people confidently make assumptions that misinterpret aro people's feelings and intentions. Romantic relationships are culturally valued as the pinnacle of interpersonal relationships, which translates into the extreme social pressure to enter into a romantic relationship regardless of one's intrinsic desire. An aro person might be asked out, in a friendly or positive way, and agree, because they think that romantic relationships are necessary or important.

An aro person may experience going on a date in a variety of ways, including (but not limited to) the following.

- They may not realize they're on a date.
- They might enjoy the date, with no reservations.
- They might enjoy the date but have negative associations with having to be on a date.
- They might resent that they felt pressured.
- They might feel guilty, ashamed, or confused that they aren't reacting to the date in the way society tells them they should.
- They might hate the date itself and its romantic connotations.
- They might have anxiety over potential future romance.
- They may enjoy the activities of the date but not frame it as romantic for themselves.
- They may like some aspects of the date but dislike others (perhaps because some aspects are more explicitly romantic).
- They might feel a romantic connection, because aromanticism is a spectrum.

Amatonormative pressure can lead to an aro person searching for ways to experience attraction, as they feel that without it they are "missing out" or "broken." The desire to have a healthy, enjoyable romantic relationship or experience can be processed by some as actual attraction. The person may not necessarily realize that they only want romance because society has taught them to want it or that they have internalized it as a necessary part of happiness. It is important to separate what the person thinks will make them happy based on what they've been taught and what the person actually wants to pursue based on their own intrinsic desires.

> *"I'm currently questioning if I'm aro and I find [it] a lot more difficult, because having a romantic relationship is something that's been ingrained in my heart as something I should strive for."*—Luiza

> *"I found it easier to identify as asexual than it was to identify as aromantic. I was in denial for a few years and resisted identifying that way. Romance is such a large part of our society. Almost everything seems designed around couples and family units. I didn't want to identify as aromantic because I was scared about what that would mean for my future. I was also terrified of being seen as lacking something people consider to be a fundamental human experience.*
>
> *It was easier to me to explain not being attracted to people sexually than it was to explain my lack of interest in a romantic partner."*—Amy

OUR ADVICE
- Educate yourself and others, especially alloromantic people, about amatonormativity and how it affects everyone.
- Know that amatonormativity exists in specific ways within individual cultures, and it is possible to participate in your culture while being true to your aromanticism and resisting amatonormativity.

- Be wary of common phrases such as "more than friends" or "at least/still having love for friends," which re-establish romantic partnership and love as the default.
- Remember that you are not broken; your boundaries, desires, and needs are legitimate; and you do not need societal approval.
- Work to design a life that will be fulfilling without the pressures of amatonormativity.
- Know that your aro identity is valid regardless of any previous or continuing experiences with romance, negative or positive.

Experiences with Partnering

In the same way that many ace people assume that their desires and experiences regarding sex disqualify them from identifying on the asexual spectrum, many aro people mistake their romantic experiences, or their desire to engage in romantic-coded actions, for proof they are not aromantic. Aro people can enjoy and partake in emotional and physical intimacy if they so choose, within non-romantic or romantic relationships. Aromanticism is defined by most to be based on lack of romantic attraction, rather than lack of romantic behavior, so being in a romantic relationship does not invalidate an aro identity.

Aro people may desire partnership for many reasons, including the presence of other attractions, emotional intimacy, coparenting, cohabiting, and financial or legal benefits. Some aro people will enter into traditional romantic relationships due to their comfort with behaviors generally coded as romantic. Other aro people will not have any interest in romance but will still enter another form of partnership. In the community, these non-romantic partnerships are often referred to as "queerplatonic," indicating that while they are like friendships, they "queer" the concept of friendship by including a level of intimacy and commitment that society considers atypical for non-romantic relationships. Not everyone who enters into a non-romantic partnership will refer to it as a queerplatonic one. There are myriad ways these partnerships may manifest, and they may not follow traditional monogamous structures. Some of these partnerships may include sex while others will not.

> *"I also found it hard to consider myself arospec having had a romantic relationship and not being opposed to having more. Surely, I thought, this must be only for people who can eschew romantic relationships entirely!"—Rowan*

> *"Accepting that I was aro was a bit harder, because I was still in a romantic relationship and didn't want to let my partner down. During my research on asexuality, I had learned about aromanticism for the first time, and I had immediately connected with it, but if I had let myself accept that I was aromantic, then that would be like admitting to myself that my whole relationship was a lie, and I wasn't ready to do that."—TB*

OUR ADVICE

- Understand that romantic feelings are often extremely difficult to define for many people, regardless of orientation, and are highly subjective. You can determine whether your feelings are romantic, platonic, alterous, some combination, or something else entirely.
- It is alright not to classify your relationships or feelings and leave them nebulous and open to interpretation.
- Familiarize yourself with other words aro communities use to describe various experiences, such as "aroflux," "romance-repulsed," and "romance-favorable."
- Know that engaging in romantic behaviors does not disqualify you from being aro.

- Consider the kinds of relationships that are possible and which ones you might want.
- It's okay to change your mind or to learn more over time about what you do or don't desire in regard to partnering.

Aro and Ace Experiences
Fear of Pathologization

Because of our amatonormative and sex-compulsory society, it is typical for aspects of ace or aro identities to be seen as "symptoms" that must be "cured." Both laypeople and health-care professionals might try to diagnose aro and ace people. For instance, people might automatically assume that aromantic people have:

- trauma over past romantic encounters or relationships
- anxiety about relationships
- an inability to connect with others, a neurodivergent personality, or a mental disorder
- lack of exposure to good relationships, especially during their upbringing
- a fear of commitment or intimacy
- insecurity, anxiety, or low self-esteem.

Asexual people might be assumed to have:

- a history of trauma, particularly sexual trauma
- a hormone imbalance
- a neurodivergent personality or mental disorder
- a lack of libido or desire caused by medication or depression
- a fear of sex caused by religious upbringing or purity culture

- insecurity, anxiety, or low self-esteem.

This pathologization is also complicated by the fact that any ace or aro person can experience any of the things listed above and may consider it relevant to their orientation. Many aro or ace people may have internalized the belief that their orientation has a cause and assume that there is something "wrong" with them. Others might be afraid of being pathologized, not just by their doctors but by their friends and family, if they embrace an ace or aro identity, and that fear could be powerful enough for them to shy away from it.

Many of the assumptions and stereotypes listed here are based in ableism and sanism, the pervasive societal mistrust and prejudice against those who are disabled, neurodivergent, or have mental health conditions. Aro and ace people are not immune from holding ableist and sanist views, and often resist accepting their orientation because they associate it with conditions denigrated by society. Even the affirming language around being asexual or aromantic is often ableist, such as reassuring someone that they are not "broken" or do not have a medical condition. After all, this still assumes that there is something wrong with having a medical condition. It is important that while resisting pathologization, aros and aces (and allies) do not use ableist frameworks, and we encourage you to learn from disabled ace and aro people and disability justice movements.

> *"I remember not responding positively to sexual encounters I had, going so far as to research if I might have a disease that was hurting me."—Laura W*

OUR ADVICE

- If you think your orientation is unrelated to other aspects of your life or health, don't second-guess yourself and ignore anyone who would suggest otherwise.

- Know that orientation doesn't need to have a cause.
- If you think there is a specific medical or psychological cause for your orientation, know that that is also valid (and there are communities who will welcome you).
- If you are in treatment or counseling, and a professional uses aspects of your orientation as a benchmark for whether or not the treatment is working, find a better person for the job.
- Remember that all people are complex, and it is next to impossible to ascribe cause to any individual part of who someone is.

Thinking Identities are All or Nothing

The simplest definition of asexuality is the lack of sexual attraction, and the simplest definition of aromanticism is the lack of romantic attraction. Therefore, some people might not think they can claim the "ace" or "aro" labels because they have only heard the simplified definition, and they have felt attraction. However the identities are more complex than that. There are many aro and ace people who identify as grayromantic or graysexual and are still part of the community.[2]

Graysexuality or grayromanticism is meant to be vague enough to allow a variety of people to identify with it. The specificity of the gray label or some other aro or ace microlabel allows someone to signal that they are on the spectrum between aromantic and alloromantic, or between asexual and allosexual, without falling on the far ends of the spectrum. Here are some reasons people might identify with grayness:

---

2   See "Asexuality and Aromanticism as Complex Identities" in Chapter 1 for more information on other ace and aro identities.

- They have experienced attraction in a few instances but not as often as their allo peers have.
- They experience an attraction that is not concrete or definitive.
- They experience attraction without desire.
- They experience desire without attraction.
- They are unsure if what they feel is attraction.
- They have some other experience that causes a dis-identification with their allo peers and some form of bond with the aro or ace community.
- They feel some disidentification with aromanticism or asexuality but not enough to disengage with the community entirely.

Not all of the reasons one might identify with a gray label can be covered here as it is meant to allow people to identify with the spectrum rather than a specific location on it. Gray can also be used as an umbrella term for various identities on the ace and aro spectrums—for example, someone who identifies as quoiromantic may identify as grayromantic as well, even if their identity is specifically quoiromantic.

> *"I think that the more I learn about asexuality, the more I see that I might be somewhere on a spectrum rather than yes/no."*—Erik

OUR ADVICE

- If you feel a partial connection to aro or ace identities, consider learning more about graysexual and grayro-mantic identities.
- Seek out narratives of grayromantic and graysexual people. See the Appendix for more.
- Know that you can identify in whatever way makes you

feel the most comfortable, whether that is identifying as asexual, aromantic, graysexual, grayromantic, with a particular microlabel, or none of the above.

- Understand that you don't need to meet certain requirements in order to identify with any aro or ace identity.
- Know that even if the definition of any particular term does describe your experience, you are not obligated to use that label if you don't want to.

The Distinction Between Ace and Aro Identities

Many people erroneously believe that asexuality is synonymous with aromanticism. In fact, these two spectrums are completely separate, and many do not identify with both asexuality and aromanticism. A pervasive misconception is that there exists one, all-encompassing form of attraction which includes romantic, sexual, aesthetic, sensual, and emotional attraction, among others. Straight people are assumed to be heterosexual and heteroromantic, just as gay people are assumed to be homosexual and homoromantic. However, that assumption does not work for a lot of aro and ace people who are not both aro *and* ace (it also does not work for all people with allosexual alloromantic orientations either, but we are focusing on aro and ace people in this book). It is therefore important to acknowledge that romantic or sexual attraction does not imply any other kind of attraction, and to allow individuals to define the boundaries between the concepts of sex and romance in their own personalized way.

> *"With being biromantic when I found out about that it was like a weight lifted off my shoulders. I always knew that I liked both guys and girls, but I didn't know that I could with being asexual. I felt like by being bi I couldn't be asexual, so I was doubting myself a lot."*—Zen

Even people who know that not all ace people are aro still may think that all aro people are ace. The aro community was formed by members of the ace community coming up with terminology to describe their aromanticism. This means that many resources on aromanticism portray aromanticism as a subset of asexuality or are asexual-centric. At first, allosexual aromantic people coming across aromanticism would only see it in the context of asexuality, which can cause confusion for them and others.

> *"For years, I had always heard of ace and aro being a package deal, I saw people who were both, or just ace, or neither, so I thought for a long time that being ace was a prerequisite to being aro. Even after I realized that just being aro was something that people could be, the relatively few number of people who were allosexual and aromantic made it difficult to find people whose experiences matched mine."—Alex*

OUR ADVICE

- Don't conflate romantic and sexual attraction, as well as other forms of attraction.
- Find narratives from aro and ace people so that you can learn more about how romantic and sexual attraction manifest in others' lives. If possible, try to find narratives from people who share multiple identities with you.
- Consistently remember to separate the terms asexual and aromantic, and never conflate the two identities.
- Remember, and remind others, particularly allos, that aromanticism and asexuality are different identities.
- Know that you and others may have different classifications of activities as "romantic" vs. "sexual" vs. "platonic," and that's okay.
- Read the "Attraction Confusion" section in Chapter 4.

Experiencing a Shift in Orientation

Occasionally, people will experience a shift in their sexual or romantic orientation. This is different than someone realizing that a label they previously used to describe themself wasn't the right fit. Sometimes the underlying feelings themselves change.

This can happen because of trauma, a medical symptom, or a side effect from a medical treatment. Other times there isn't a specific cause that can be identified. Many people find that regardless of how they became aromantic or asexual, it is their lived reality now, and so they choose to take on the label. They may experience a shift back to their prior orientation at a later date and they may not. Those who have this experience might struggle with whether or not they are allowed to identify as asexual or aromantic and might be unsure if they want to. However, experiencing a shift in identities is valid and all identities, old and new, are also valid.

> *"I do remember being what people call 'allo,' I guess. I always had a crush on some boy or another in middle and high school, and I remember having a more active sex drive, though I didn't lose my virginity until I was almost 19. I used to tell people I was straighter than an arrow. But I think once I hit about 17, 18, that changed. I don't think any one thing changed it, really; I just lost my drive. I do have depression, and I'm sure that was part of it. But it never felt like there was something wrong, it was just kind of a thing that happened."—Hannah*

> *"I think that my orientation changed over time, I used to be bisexual and it just faded away into ace over time. When I realized that I was ace, I thought it was just a lull in my libido and would pass, then it was gone for a week, then a month, then a year... I finally fully accepted it about a year and a half after realizing that I had almost no sex drive."—Nightingale*

OUR ADVICE

- Never invalidate others' labels, whether or not they seem consistent with past labels; instead, accept them for how they define themselves in the present.
- If you are struggling with changing your own labels, remember that identities are meant to be descriptive, not prescriptive, and are used to define how you currently feel rather than being declarations that you will always feel the same way in the future.
- Understand that people are complex and can change over time, and it is not a "betrayal" to a previously held identity to redefine yourself.
- Know that changing identities does not mean there is something wrong with you, nor does it make prior and future identities any less valid.

History of Trauma

Some ace and aro people are assumed to have experienced a traumatic event that "caused" their ace or aro identity. Consequently, their orientation is then dismissed as illegitimate by skeptics around them. Those skeptics may believe that aro and ace people need to be healed from their trauma, which would result in the ability to feel the attractions or desires they lack. Some aro or ace people have experienced sexual violence, intimate partner violence, physical trauma, traumatic break-ups, or other trauma in their lives, but many have not. The assumption that they have experienced trauma can lead them to try to find non-existent trauma. Also, even when trauma has occurred, sometimes it may be entirely unrelated to their orientation.

> "My dad suggested that it was 'a phase' and questioned what 'caused' me to become ace."—Becca

There are also aro and ace people whose identity has been impacted in some way by a history of sexual, romantic, or emotional trauma. Some people will have had a different orientation before the trauma and may have noticed a change in their orientation after the fact. Others may have experienced trauma at a young age and not have a frame of reference for whether their trauma impacted their orientation. These ace and aro people may worry that their experience with trauma means they aren't really ace or aro, or that they are perpetuating the stereotype of trauma causing asexuality or aromanticism. Aro and ace people are allowed to identify as aro or ace because of the trauma, and their identity is just as valid.

It's important to know that trauma does sometimes cause aromanticism or asexuality, and that's okay. Curing asexuality and aromanticism is not a part of recovery. Alloromanticism and allosexuality are not necessary components of one's life or health.

> *"It took me almost two years to fully accept being asexual after realizing it because of past experiences like rape and being in relationships and faking heterosexual behavior."*—DasTenna

OUR ADVICE

- If someone identifies as aro or ace, never question why they do—just accept it as you would accept any other orientation.
- If you have suffered trauma, know that working through that doesn't require changing your orientation(s).
- If you want to explore the link between your orientation and your trauma, you can, but know you do not need to be unhappy with your orientation nor want to change your orientation to do so.

- Understand that it is perfectly valid to identify as ace or aro even if you have experienced trauma, and you aren't confirming stereotypes of asexuality or aromanticism.
- While orientations can shift at any time and for a variety of reasons, and therefore may shift during therapeutic interventions, that should not be a goal or expected.
- Refer to the Appendix for a list of resources for ace and aro survivors of trauma.

Influences of Other Identities

The process of embracing an aromantic or asexual orientation is complicated by other social and political identities, including race, ethnicity, religion, gender, ability, body type, health, neurotype, location, class, age, and other LGBTQIA+ identities. Nobody can identify their orientation in a vacuum, and everyone is influenced by societal expectations and stereotypes. Some groups are hypersexualized, while others are desexualized. There are also some demographics that are seen as or expected to be highly romantic and some that are excluded from romantic consideration or are seen as incapable of romance. These external assumptions can be internalized in a way that creates uncertainty and doubt when first grappling with aro and ace orientations.

> *"As a Mexican woman everyone expects me to be very flirty and sexy."—Mariel*

All of these ideas can make self-identifying as ace or aro much more difficult. Here are a few examples.

- An East Asian man who identifies as asexual may worry that he is simply playing into societal expectations of him and that his orientation is less legitimate.
- An allosexual aromantic white woman who feels

society expects her to only want or have sex within a romantic relationship may think of herself as "broken" or "dirty" in some way.

- An autistic agender person may think that ze does not relate sexually or romantically towards others because of zer autism and may not feel that ze can identify as aroace.

- A woman with severe cerebral palsy may feel uncomfortable identifying as asexual, even if she does not experience sexual attraction, due to how her peers and care providers have desexualized and infantilized her over the course of her life.

- A 60-year-old married man may not want to upend his long-time stable relationship by exploring that he does not have romantic feelings towards his spouse.

- A devout Christian aromantic allosexual person may force themself into a traditional romantic relationship, and even get married, believing that acting on sexual desire outside a relationship is sinful.

- An asexual gay man may have a history of engaging in sexual activity without desiring it because he feels it is expected of him, both by his partners and by society at large.

The difficulty of coming to terms with aro or ace identity can be confounded when your other established identity groups do not have strong aro or ace representation or are actively represented in ways that seem contradictory to aro or ace identity. It can be difficult to find support for one's specific experience, and a person may end up feeling distanced from all of their peer groups due to the seemingly conflicting identities. Some people feel like they must eventually "pick a side," and choose one identity that matters more than the others in order to fit into at least one community.

"Religion made me think that I was blessed to be able to save it for marriage. Religion made me feel shame for porn and masturbation. It didn't allow me to examine what I was into or not into. It asserted that anything not 'straight' is wrong and did not exist as anything more than a choice. I didn't even consider why I didn't want sex until after I got out of it. Then I realized that I still didn't want to have sex."—Samuel B

"My experiences as an Asian male is that society doesn't really see me as a sexual being by default. It's more being invisible than being less attractive. I don't attribute it entirely to racism. That's too simple. There is a cultural difference between my Asian side and my American side that has to be crossed. And most of my Asian friends prefer to date within the race.

Before I accepted my low sex drive, I felt obligated to socialize and flirt with women. The first barrier I had to overcome was signaling that I was interested in dating outside my race. And I sometimes perceive a switch in how non-Asian women behave towards me when they realize I might be interested in them."—Anonymous

OUR ADVICE

- You can find others who have similar intersecting identities, as sharing those experiences may be helpful—while it may be hard to find people in person, there are many resources available online.
- Understand that society's assumptions about you based on your identity do not have to change how you identify.
- Know that you do not have to be a "good representative" or token of any of your communities and that you are not responsible for how other people stereotype you or your communities.

- Embrace all your different and intersecting identities—we know it can be more difficult to be a minority within a minority, but we're glad you're here.

Disidentification with the LGBTQIA+ Community

Some people may experience a lack of sexual or romantic attraction, acknowledge this lack, and still not identify as ace or aro. Sometimes this is due to either holding negative perceptions of people with non-straight orientations or being afraid of being subjected to those same negative perceptions from others. Others also might not identify with the broader LGBTQIA+ community, even if they do identify with an ace or aro orientation. Some people may feel like the community emphasizes queer attraction and thus feel alienated because they do not identify with that experience.

> *"I don't view myself as being part of the LGBTQ+ community due to personal reasons and lack of connection. I support the community and those on the aro/ace spectrum that want to belong and crave the resources the community has to offer, but I personally wouldn't benefit from meeting people from this community. I often get the feeling that people who aren't on the ace/aro spectrum don't want to discuss my identity or understand it, no matter how close we are. I simply do not feel safe talking about my issues with people who aren't ace/aro to the core or show[ing] major support for these identities and therefore I only count myself as being part of the aspec/ace community."—Sara S*

Other times this disidentification is because they experience hetero-attraction in some form (like someone who might identify as aromantic and heterosexual). They may feel more of a connection to the attraction that they do experience, or they may not feel like they have a right to identify with an LGBTQIA+ identity or feel that they might not be accepted.

"I think I understood the principles quite well, I just didn't initially think that asexual people were as straight-laced as me. I assumed they were very out there and alternative in their appearance and lifestyles. This is not always the case at all."—*Lilly*

OUR ADVICE

- Know that not all ace or aro people identify with the LGBTQIA+ community and that you don't need to either.
- On the other hand, many aro and ace people do identify with the LGBTQIA+ community, and you are welcome to do so! We (along with agender people) are the "A" in this acronym, after all.
- If you experience heteroromantic or heterosexual attraction and are also ace or aro, you are still welcome in the LGBTQIA+ community if you choose to be a part of it. You can call yourself straight or not, whatever makes you more comfortable; straight and queer are not mutually exclusive.
- You can try to process internalized negative associations with LGBTQIA+ communities, if you think you have them. (Note: this does not mean you need to then identify as LGBTQIA+.)
- LGBTQIA+ spaces are not immune from all kinds of prejudices and systems of oppression, and you don't need to force yourself to stay somewhere you feel unsafe.
- Exclusionism is not universal, and there are many

LGBTQIA+ communities who welcome aro and ace people, regardless of any other identities they hold.

Gatekeeping

Unfortunately, there is a common problem of people being told by others that they are not allowed to identify as ace or aro. Sometimes this comes from within the ace and aro communities, for example:

- "You can't be asexual if you have sex."
- "You can't be aromantic if you aren't asexual."

Other times this can come from the broader LGBTQIA+ community or beyond, for example:

- "Asexuality isn't real."
- "Aromantic people don't need to be part of the LGBTQIA+ community. You aren't oppressed the way we are."
- "Asexual people shouldn't come to larger LGBTQIA+ meetings, since they aren't looking to hook up with anyone anyway."
- "Aro and ace people have straight-passing privilege, so they shouldn't invade queer spaces."

People who identify with "gray" labels are often harassed by people both inside and outside aro and ace communities. Some people ask why graysexual and grayromantic people are part of the aspec communities. They may even suggest that these are simply allosexual or alloromantic people who want to feel "special" or "unique." After all, many who identify as alloromantic only feel romantic attraction for friends or after they've formed an emotional bond with their future partners, like demiromantic people. There are also sex-repulsed allosexual people who may have the same experiences as aegosexual people, who don't want to or can't imagine themselves participating in sexual scenarios. However, the ace and aro communities generally feel very strongly that as all of these feelings are subjective, every individual must decide for themselves where one identity starts and another ends.

> *"Part of my denial was also coming from the backlash that ace people suffered online during the period I was still questioning myself. I didn't want to be part of the group that was being mocked, and maybe I wasn't even an actual ace, since the parts of asexuality that resonated with me were being questioned by purists and exclusionists alike. It's a little bit ironic how Tumblr both helped me and stopped me from identifying as ace."—Elena*

OUR ADVICE

- Understand that these gatekeeping statements are not accurate and don't represent the majority's opinion.
- You can find communities that are accepting.
- If this kind of gatekeeping impacts your confidence in your identity, feel free to disengage from people and communities who are negatively affecting you.

CHAPTER 7

Part Four—Exploration and Education

It is almost impossible for aro and ace people to explore their communities without becoming more educated about the aromantic and asexual spectrums, and it is equally difficult to learn more about those identities without engaging, even passively, with their communities.[1]

Writers of fictional stories are often aware of a simple, classic adage: "Show, don't tell." When a hypothetical person named Ris begins to realize asexuality or aromanticism is a possible identity for them, they will likely first search for resources that "tell" them about asexuality or aromanticism. Ris will read definitions of the terms, bullet lists of what asexuality or aromanticism is and is not, see glossaries of related terms, and perhaps look at a few graphs or charts. They will see the abstract theoretical framework and realize they might fit somewhere in there—but they also might not know yet if they fit. Ris may need to hear or read fleshed-out narratives and anecdotes with specific details before they can truly start to connect with an ace or aro identity.

Especially with the dearth of media representations, coming

---

1   Chapter 2 is about the history of the ace and aro communities, their cultures, and how to engage with them.

across other aro and ace people in community spaces who are sharing their personal stories would likely be the first time Ris has ever encountered a story of this nature. Through interacting with aro and ace communities, they can slowly start to understand asexuality and aromanticism as complex human identities—as frameworks that explain many different and subtle facets of aces' and aros' experiences.

Through these personal narratives, community members "show":

- what being aro or ace means during specific interpersonal interactions
- how it emotionally feels to be ace or aro in society
- how aromanticism or asexuality helps retrospectively explain earlier life experiences
- how the lives of ace and aro people change after joining communities and adopting their specific identity labels.

"I was pretty involved in one forum for a while and it helped me solidify my beliefs about asexuality and other LGBTQ+ identities. I don't think I would have come to the conclusion that I am asexual without the online communities and support, just people sharing their stories and being able to relate to them helped me a lot."—Lauren H

For many aro and ace people, interacting with others' narratives is an important part of exploring their identity and learning more about what it means to be ace or aro.

This does not come without risk. As we said in Chapter 2, asexual and aromantic communities are not free from racism, ableism, sexism, homophobia, transphobia, and other bigoted perspectives. If you belong to a marginalized group, you may face these harmful attitudes when joining these communities.

Unfortunately, there is no guarantee you will find a space without these bigots. However, there are spaces that work hard to lift up the voices of marginalized aro and ace people, and you can also find others who share your background or identity and listen to their stories as well. As we mentioned previously, you do not need to stay or participate in spaces where you feel unsafe.

Asexual/Aromantic Communities
Online

An online community is, the vast majority of the time, the first aro or ace community a person will come across. It is also worth noting that in order to search for and discover in-person, offline communities, the majority of aro and ace people must use websites such as meetup.com or other online sources. Without access to the internet, an ace or aro person would have a slim chance of stumbling across an in-person community.

Different people have different preferences when it comes to choosing which sites provide community spaces that feel comfortable, safe, and enjoyable. One big, 20-year-old hub of the asexual community is the AVEN forums, a message board on asexuality.org. A few years ago, a forum for aros was created—Arocalypse. It was not the first aro forum, but it is the most successful one so far. Other forums that have been relatively popular for aces are specific-language forums for non-English speaking aces. Some non-English forums are associated with AVEN while others are independent.

While some prefer forums, many are not comfortable in such spaces. Instead, they have found and prefer communities on Reddit, Facebook, Discord Servers, Skype IM chats, Google Hangout IM chats, LiveJournal, Dreamwidth, Pillowfort, blogs, Instagram, Twitter, Tumblr, and YouTube. On many of these websites, people might "follow" or "subscribe to" each other in various ways, and large groups of people might all follow the same groups of content creators.

It can be intimidating to engage with online communities, especially when questioning orientations. It is completely understandable and valid to be afraid of posting personal content online, particularly about something as intimate as orientation. The sheer amount of content already posted can also be daunting, particularly when first engaging with aro and ace communities. Some content will be extremely specific and may not be relevant to each individual, such as narratives about the intersection of asexuality and mental illness or what it is like being aromantic and nonbinary. Other content is highly nuanced; intra-community debates may not make much sense unless someone is already immersed. Consider, for example, the debate around how to define and use the term "platonic." (See Chapter 1 for the definition and more details.) Still more posts may not be interesting or helpful to someone focused on understanding their identity, such as theories about aromantic or asexual characters in pop culture.

There are also some accessibility issues with some platforms that can make it difficult to engage with them. Some are difficult for people with neurodivergence, particularly attention deficit disorder (ADD) or attention deficit hyperactivity disorder (ADHD), to process. Others are particularly difficult for people with visual impairments and who need to use screen readers, especially given the reliance on emojis and keysmashes online and the frequent images without descriptions.

Due to the publicity of some of these platforms, they may also expose one to derogatory statements from people outside of the community. Some sites have become well known for hosting large sects of people who are unaccepting of ace and aro identities. Some of these people would fall into the category of "internet trolls," while others are even more malicious. Some skew towards the side of harmful memes and humor about ace and aro people; others treat their stance as a staunch political view concerning the LGBTQ+ community. This vitriol can also come from inside the community and is generally directed at those who relate to their identities in a different manner or identify with labels that are less accepted. These attitudes and behaviors are harmful to ace and aro people who are trying to connect with those similar to them and create community bonds.

> *"I am not active in any aro community, because it's hard to find one that fits me. I find a lot of aro communities are full of aro-ace people, so our experiences don't always fit well. Because how I experience attraction to people revolves so heavily around friendship and sex, it's sometimes hard to share my feelings to a group that contains aro-aces who are sex-repulsed. I don't want to make anyone else uncomfortable, but it's very difficult to find a group that is strictly aromantics, where everyone still experiences sexual attraction."—Alex*

OUR ADVICE

- Know that there are many ways to join online communities. There are also different levels of engagement, and you can participate in the way that is most comfortable to you.
- Read, watch, and generally engage with others' content! Simply consuming content can be tremendously helpful in exploring identity, and you do not have any obligation to post anything yourself.
- If you would like to contribute without creating your own content, there is nothing wrong with simply commenting on or reblogging others' content, such as their fanfiction, YouTube videos, or personal essays, and many creators would appreciate this engagement.
- Do not engage with trolls. It is perfectly fine to block

anyone and to report people who are breaking the terms of service of the community.

- Know that you deserve to experience online spaces comfortably, free from online harassment, and that you do not have to "tough it out."
- If you encounter problematic or upsetting discourse, take a step back from it.
- Visit forums like AVEN or Arocalypse to find information about topics of interest. For more resources, check the Appendix.
- Within online communities, you can seek out other aro and ace people who share additional identities and interests with you.

In Person

As the number of in-person ace communities has grown, especially in large cities and on college and university campuses, the likelihood that someone's first experience with an ace community will be offline has increased. However, there are still relatively few in-person aromanticism-specific communities, leading most aros to the internet rather than offline communities. A handful of in-person groups welcome both ace and aro people, including aromantic allosexual people, but more commonly ace groups welcome ace people, some of whom also happen to be aro. This exclusion of aromantic people who do not identify as ace may be accidental, incidental, or implicit. Regardless, their exclusion leads many aro people who are not ace to feel there is no in-person community for them. There are not nearly enough aro or ace in-person communities.

In order to get involved in offline ace or aro communities, all you need to do is "show up." Deciding to show up is the hardest step, but there are many options—a meetup.com event, a pride parade, or a conference—and you can choose the setting or settings that are the best fit for you.

> *"I want a community in person. I would love to go to maybe a support group once in a while or a dinner or find literature or something to make me feel like I belong. I know there are people online and they have been great! But I don't want to be in front of a screen all the time in order to find community."*—Anonymous

It is often intimidating to take the step from online searching and interactions to finding and attending groups in person. Consider a hypothetical demiromantic, demisexual person named Jasina. She courageously decides to find an ace group in their city, but she may be worried about outing herself the first time she attends. Just showing up to the meetup implies that she is ace, and there is no way to hide that from their fellow attendees. If allies are welcome, which is only true at some ace meetup groups, Jasina might feel less inherently outed by coming to the meetup because she can portray herself as an ally.

On the other hand, there are many in-person groups that do not invite allies, which can provide a safer environment for Jasina to come out, since she knows everyone at this group is ace too. Still, coming out, even in a supportive environment, is a big step that can be anxiety inducing for anyone. Additionally, if Jasina is still questioning her orientation, if she has internalized anti-demi/anti-gray sentiments, or if she has reason to fear gatekeeping of demi or gray individuals, she may feel that she would not be welcome at an ace meetup or that going would say something about her that might not be true.

Another compounding factor is the intersection with mental health and neurodivergence. A large number of aro and ace people have anxiety, depression, or other mental health issues, or are autistic or neurodivergent. Feeling social anxiety, being socially withdrawn, or socializing in a non-neurotypical way can make going to an in-person meeting, especially with new people who may already know each other, very intimidating.

OUR ADVICE

- Look online to find groups that meet locally. See the Appendix for a list of resources on these groups.
- If you choose to attend an in-person meeting but do not want to speak about any personal experiences, that is okay! You can always share as much or as little as you'd like.
- If you are questioning or are unsure of your identity, you are still welcome at in-person meetings. You do not need to be sure about your identity in order to be "allowed" to attend.
- If you are nervous about attending an in-person meeting, you can start by choosing an introductory meeting; many in-person groups have regular meetings for new people, where anyone can come and engage as much as they feel comfortable.
- If you are feeling anxious about attending a meeting, you can private message one of the group's organizers and ask any questions you have. Most organizers are very friendly and eager to alleviate concerns, and they want to make sure that the meeting will be safe, comfortable, and welcoming for everyone who attends.

Passive vs. Active Engagement

There are different methods for interacting with the ace and aro communities. Some are more passive, such as reading through forums and blog posts and listening without speaking during meetings. People can be more active in the community by actively speaking, writing, and contributing in community spaces. Whether a person participates passively or actively will depend on their own understanding of and comfort with their identity, as well as their personality, ability, and amount of time they can spend.

> *"I only have so much social energy in me. But what time I do spend in those spaces is really helpful in normalizing the experience in general. Hearing other people's experiences helps me figure out how to answer questions better in my own life, should they come up."—Kathryn S*

Some people engage passively by consuming media that they connect to[2]—that could be media with explicitly aro or ace characters, like Todd Chavez from *BoJack Horseman* or Clover from *The Last 8* by Laura Pohl. Others may enjoy media with subtextual aro or ace representation, like Keladry from Tamora Pierce's *Protector of the Small* series or Sherlock Holmes. Finding connections through fictional characters can be extremely cathartic and affirming, and carries less risk than interacting with people. It can also be a safe space to think about and explore identity, through headcanons or writing fanfic.

Engaging passively is just as legitimate as engaging actively. Passive engagement still counts as participation within the community and can still be beneficial to the psyche of the person engaging. Engaging more actively can allow greater control over the content and experiences one is seeing and can help guide community discussion in a way that is more personally helpful. Engaging more passively can be less physically and mentally straining, can allow exploration of identity without inviting prying questions on your experiences, and can help one feel less alone. Engagement exists on a spectrum from passive to active; some people may feel comfortable liking and sharing content but not talking or writing about their own experiences. Others may be able to add comments, without starting a conversation themselves. Which types of participation feel passive vs. active will vary between different individuals.

---

2   See "Aro and Ace Representation in Media" in Chapter 2.

"I follow ace blogs on Tumblr and Facebook, I read all the articles I can find on the subject, but I don't actively participate. This is enough for me right now—I just need that reassurance that other people have similar experiences and questions to mine."—Torie

OUR ADVICE

- Consider the benefits of different kinds of engagement and what you are comfortable doing.
- Intentionally choose where and how to engage.
- Know that whatever way you choose to engage is perfectly fine.
- Do not feel pressure to participate in any way that you don't want to, especially if it involves sharing details about your thoughts or experiences. You do not owe anyone any part of yourself or your identity.

Results of Engaging in Ace and Aro Communities

As discussed in Chapter 4, many ace and aro people feel lonely and isolated because they have no connection to other people who have similar experiences or perspectives in relation to sex or romance. Joining an ace or aro community, whether offline or online, often reduces these feelings of isolation. Most aro and ace people feel that outside of these communities, society doesn't know they exist, would shun them if it did, or, at the very least, does not remember or care to include them. But even if they only enter these spaces to see aro- and ace-themed memes and pride art, it makes most aces and aros feel fortunate, and relieved, to have access to such a community.

In these communities, there is a reprieve from societal pressures and expectations around sexuality and romance, which can help an aro or ace person clarify and address their own feelings about relationships. They can also recontextualize their past experiences through comparison to others', which can allow them to determine whether some events and feelings were due to their orientation.

> *"I think online communities and the positivity there really did help a lot; realizing that I wasn't alone, that there was nothing wrong with me, was really helpful."—Aeden*

Aro and ace people can also start reimagining their futures with the help of a community. If Yousef is an allosexual aromantic person, they may not have ever thought that they could have long-term sexual relationships without romance. However, they may meet Minh, who is in a long-term sexual relationship with a friend without romance. Yousef now has a model for one way forward in their life. These communities give new-comers an opportunity to reframe their lives free from society's amatonormative and sex-compulsory expectations. They also enable people to hear about others' dreams for their futures or about various living situations and relationships that are counter-culture and work towards building something similar for themselves.

Conversely, some aro and ace individuals feel comfortable enough with their identity and settled enough into their lives that they do not see the point of engaging with communities. These aces and aros might not frame what they did when they first learned about the asexual spectrum or the aromantic spectrum as "participating in" a community; nonetheless, many of them did read narratives from the ace and aro community before deciding a particular identity label fit comfortably.

Sadly, there are very real risks to engaging with communities. People may have alienating experiences in specific aro or ace community spaces. Ideally, they can recover from the negative experience and find a different ace or aro space where they feel more comfortable participating. Unfortunately, some aro or ace people act in exclusionary ways, such as saying that if one engages in a particular romantic or sexual activity or has a particular desire, they're not "ace" or not "aro" enough. Some online ace or aro community hubs are places where arophobic or acephobic people may see intra-community conversation or content—and then, as an outsider, express bigotry towards the aros and aces who are simply trying to enjoy their community space. Communities can also contain negative things that are neither specifically ace nor specifically aro related, such as racism, ableism, and other bigotries. These bigoted actions can be very harmful to aro or ace people's online experience and discovery journey. Cyberbullying and harassment are severe issues online, and LGBTQIA+ communities, as well as smaller aro and ace spaces, are not exempt from this behavior. As ace and aro communities are small, and often overlap, it can be difficult to escape a bad experience, and this can also be a hindrance to people hoping to engage with others. It can be particularly frustrating when these debates escalate from simple conversations over the semantics of identity terminology into harassment or when misstatements are taken as proof of bigotry.

However, most ace and aro people find that the benefits outweigh the risks, which include gaining a greater understanding and acceptance of inherent parts of themselves as well as the tools to overcome feelings of shame, confusion, and denial. Often, real, deep friendships are formed through both online and offline communities. These friendships are powerful and important to many ace and aro people, especially those who struggle to connect with others who are not aro or ace on certain topics. Furthermore, joining communities often provides a safe space for aro and ace people to have a social outlet.

"I talk daily on the Aromantic and Asexual Spectrum Discord Server since I first started identifying as aromantic, which was *just a week before I started identifying as asexual too. Having that community to talk to and make friends in has been great. It's so much fun to learn about attraction and everything, hear people's experiences and tease out fine details about this from new people's questions. It's really helped me feel a part of the asexual and aromantic community. I've met some of my closest online friends there and care a lot about so many of the people I've met over the past roughly year and a half. It makes me happy to be asexual and aromantic and to know there are so many other people like me."—Anonymous*

Other LGBTQIA+ Communities

Sometimes, where there isn't a local or welcoming ace or aro community, a larger LGBTQIA+ community can help ace and aro individuals in a similar way. When first exploring their identities, many aro or ace people may identify as another, non-heterosexual identity. If Jisoo is an aromantic asexual person, they may think that they are bisexual at first, since they feel the same level of sexual and romantic attraction to all genders. However, after meeting some people who are bisexual, Jisoo can compare experiences and realize that what they had understood as equal attraction to all genders was actually zero attraction to all genders and that bisexual is not the best label for them. Meeting other LGBTQIA+ people can help Jisoo better define themself, if only by eliminating some identities from contention. Jisoo may also be able to find other ace or aro people who joined the group for the same reason and connect with those peers.

Even if Jisoo is comfortable in their identity, and there are no other aro or ace people in this group, it can be helpful just to compare experiences with other LGBTQIA+ people. While there are obvious differences between identifying as aro and ace and identifying with another LGBTQIA+ orientation, there are many similarities as well.[3] It can help aro and ace people to hear the stories of other LGBTQIA+ people. For example, it is especially useful to see the ways that other people defy the hetero- and cisnormative societal narrative and demonstrate the ways that all LGBTQIA+ people can create futures for themselves that they don't necessarily see represented in the mainstream.

Engaging Outside of Queer Communities

Some aro and ace people may not be ready to engage with LGBTQIA+ communities, especially if they are new. They may prefer to explore their identities by talking with family, friends, or care providers. They will almost certainly have many new and complex feelings to work through with others, and it is important that they receive the support and understanding that they need. It might be challenging, as this likely requires coming out, but it may be easier to talk about their history and identities with people who they already know.[4]

---

3   See "Asexuality and Aromanticism Compared to Other LGBTQIA+ Iden-
    tities" in Chapter 9.
4   For more on coming out, see all of Chapter 9.

CHAPTER 8

Part Five—Identity Acceptance and Salience Negotiation

In Part Five of this model, we explore the process by which aro and ace people begin to accept their identity as part of themselves and decide how important it is to them and their future. In no particular order, an aro or ace person will begin to process negative feelings, such as how they feel about past experiences of sexual or romantic trauma; distinguish what types of attractions and desires they do and do not experience; imagine a future catering to their own desires rather than external expectations; and decide how important their ace or aro identity is to their overall sense of self. Identity acceptance is not an all-or-nothing ordeal. To put it simply, someone can accept their ace or aro identity, understand it as a large part of their lives, and still be uneasy about it.

Understanding the nuances of your orientation's role in your past, present, and future is an important part of processing negative sentiments over being ace or aro. Once you are looking at a more full picture of your own life and what being this orientation means, you will have a new framework for how consequential or inconsequential being ace or aro is for your overall sense of self.

Accepting yourself is not always easy. It is a process that is greatly aided by the acquiring of skills for accepting, loving, and living with your ace and aro identities. Whether these skills come from fellow ace and aro folks, friends, family, or medical professionals, they can lift a great burden off of you coming to terms with your identity. On the flip side, there can often be negative pressure on ace and aro people to be completely certain and accepting of their identities in order to be considered valid. However, acceptance is an ongoing process that in some cases will endure for the length of your life, whether the reasons are internal or external. For many, the journey of understanding their own desires and how to craft a future around them will take years and never result in a concrete answer. Processing your past with romance, sex, your connection to your body, and other issues relevant to your orientation can also take a very long time and may never truly end.

Finding the Perfect Words for One's Orientation

While the ace and aro communities are often perceived as a single monolith, there are in fact many different variations to the identities of people within these communities. Some people may be completely comfortable with the labels "ace" or "aro" and do not need to further elaborate on or specify their experience. On the other hand, there are many different microlabels people may use, including demi, gray, lith, and more. These can help people to understand themselves, particularly in relation to other people in the community. Some of these are listed and defined in the glossary.

While choosing words and labels for their orientation, many ace and aro people take time to explore their nuances. Some people might do research into the different parts of the community to find where they fit. Since the aro and ace communities are small and relatively new, the language around ace and aro identities and how those identities may impact other aspects of oneself is constantly evolving and being redefined, and people discover and create new identities for themselves every day. For example, in 2018, the term "arogender" was coined by the Tumblr user arokaladin to mean "Any gender identity influenced by an aromantic or aromantic spectrum identity."[1] These different labels can serve to help ace and aro people find sub-communities of others with similar life experiences. Labels can also help ace and aro people more precisely understand how their identity impacts their lived experience and help them imagine what they want in their future.

> *"When I discovered more of the microlabels that fell under the umbrella of asexuality, especially aegosexuality, I felt right at home, but it took time."—Lauren*

While the focus on adopting or even inventing new microlabels may seem silly, over the top, or unnecessary to people outside the aro or ace communities, individual aro or ace people often feel that they need to understand their feelings more precisely or know exactly where they fall within the larger ace or aro communities. Being told to just accept feelings without analyzing them or trying to fit them into a broader landscape can be frustrating or feel dismissive. On the other hand, some ace and aro people do not find microlabels necessary for understanding their experiences and identity. For them, simply using "ace" or "aro" is enough—even if they could define their attraction in ways that align with a microlabel. Each person's engagement with microlabels is different, and choosing to use or not to use microlabels is a personal decision that may shift over time.

---

1   arokaladin (2018) "Kaladin Stormblessed is Romance Repulsed." Accessed on 4/5/2022 at https://web.archive.org/web/20190413014710/https://arokaladin.tumblr.com/post/173000032149/ok-here-we-go-im-coining-it-arogender-any.

There are other labels that can be helpful to understanding an aromantic or asexual identity that are more tangentially connected to orientation. For instance, within the ace community, an individual's openness to engaging in sex, with or without sexual attraction, can be explained with a few labels:

- Sex-favorable: Enjoys and potentially seeks out sex.
- Sex-neutral or sex-indifferent: Generally does not seek out sex independently, but may be comfortable engaging in sex if other conditions are met, such as arousal, being asked by a committed partner, etc.
- Sex-averse: Does not want to personally engage in sex.
- Sex-repulsed: Dislikes descriptions and depictions of sex, does not want to think about sexual activity.[2]

All of these experiences can have varying intensities, and people may respond to different depictions of sex in varying ways. For example, some people may be comfortable or even seek out hearing or reading about sex but are not comfortable seeing or participating in sexual activities.

> "I do not [watch pornography]. I had a fascination for it during puberty, then caught a glimpse of a video online and was put off by the reality of it."—Jess

The same labels exist for romance within the aro community, and these labels can be useful when thinking about potential relationships or partnerships and the activities that someone is open to participating in.

---

2   For more detailed definitions of these and many other terms, see the glossary.

Processing Negative Feelings

There are many negative feelings that aro and ace people may have to process when coming to terms with their identities. In the responses to our questionnaires, ace and aro people discussed negative feelings around their orientations, and their responses could generally fit into a few main themes, listed below.

While some or even many of those feelings may persist or reemerge throughout life, understanding, rejecting, or moving past them is an important part of embracing an ace or aro identity. Many of these experiences will overlap in category, but it can be helpful to think about them in specific contexts to better understand their impacts. Some of these experiences are similar to the roadblocks in Chapter 6 and can be overcome in the same way.

Many of the negative feelings stem from amatonormativity and compulsory sexuality, both of which impact some people and communities more than others. In particular, amatonormativity is a tool of white supremacy and the patriarchy, stigmatizing non-white and non-Western forms of relationships, as well as reinforcing toxic gender roles and attitudes.[3]

Reexamining Past Experiences and Trauma

- Feeling unworthy of romance or sex regardless of orientation or identity.
- Worried that the identity is because of physical or psychological trauma or sickness.
- Wishing to be "normal."
- Realizing that past romantic or sexual activity was not wanted or enthusiastically consented to.

---

3   For more on this, see https://taaap.org/2022/02/21/sexposcon-poster-amatonormativity. Accessed on 11/10/2022.

- Feeling guilty over engaging in sex or romance in the past without attraction.
- Realizing the existence of a whole social world that revolves around romance and sexuality for the first time.

> *"At first I definitely wished I wasn't aromantic and asexual, still do sometimes. I'd be listening to music and for the first time realize it was about romance and start crying because it was another reminder of me being different, and of how good attraction was supposed to be."*—Anonymous

The negative feelings based around past trauma and the recontextualization of previous experiences require long-term self-examination and forgiveness.[4]

OUR ADVICE

- Be kind to your past self for not having had the context or knowledge you have today.
- Remember that common experiences that may not seem generally traumatic may still be difficult for you to remember.
- Remember that an experience that is not traumatic for one aro or ace person may be traumatic for another aro or ace person, including for reasons related to historic and continued intersecting systems of oppression.
- Seek out narratives of other aro or ace people so you can see that you are not alone.
- Learn about romantic and sexual social cues and how to disentangle yourself from potentially romantic or sexual situations you don't want to be in.

---

4   The next section of this chapter discusses trauma in more depth.

- While some aspects of your past and future will remain out of your control, there are steps that you can take right now to improve your life and emotional state, such as going to therapy, joining a support group (including an ace- or aro-specific group), and engaging in self-care in whatever ways work for you.

Finding Communities/Your Place in the World Today

- Feeling guilty over not wanting sex or not wanting romance with a partner.
- Worrying about how to navigate a current intimate partnership and if a breakup is inevitable.
- Feeling left out from certain conversations with friends and family regarding sex, romance, or general life goals.
- Not feeling accepted by society (which tends to seem to be sex- and romance-obsessed).
- Not enjoying media because of lack of representation or over-representation of sexual and romantic themes.
- Annoyed with having to explain asexuality or aromanticism to everyone and being seen as a "special snowflake" or a social outcast.
- Feeling broken because romantic love and sex are purported to be the most important part of life.

"I do find being ace to have a bigger impact on my ability to connect with people in the way I'd like compared to my other identities. A lot of people are able to connect through shared sexual energy, particularly at queer and kink events. I find that type of situation really uncomfortable and have to try to connect with people in other ways. I find that to be frustrating and I sometimes wish I didn't have to deal with that."—Kira

Some of these negative feelings are rooted in the difficulty of differing from the norm and being unable to connect with peers and family as well as you would like. For these experiences, a lot can be achieved by talking to partners, friends, and family about your concerns and fears.

OUR ADVICE

- Talk to your friends and family about your identity and the way you feel left out of conversations around sex or romance. You can try practicing these conversations with a sympathetic friend, especially if they are also queer and may understand your perspective.
- Engage with media that does not include sex or romance or includes aro or ace representation. See the Appendix for some suggestions.
- Remember that you do not owe anyone your identity. You do not have to come out unless you want to.
- You deserve for your boundaries to be respected. Establish boundaries in any current partnership, if you are in one, and in other relationships you have, such as your family or friendships.
- While it may be painful, being alone is better than being disrespected or unsafe.
- If you feel that you are unable to reconcile with certain friends or family members, you do not have to reconcile with them; you can choose to end the relationships if that is a boundary that is most healthy for you. Move forward in whatever way meets your needs and find people who will be accepting and respectful of your identities.

Creating a future

- Worrying about finding a long-term relationship, whether romantic, sexual, or neither.
- Not knowing how to find a partner who will respect new-found boundaries and desires, and feeling that it may be impossible.
- Having difficulty finding other people who share the same experiences, feelings, and goals for the future, and especially finding others who identify with a microlabel.
- Worrying about how to take care of practicalities, like finances or aging family members, without the same support system most people gain through marriage.
- Grief over the loss of the future that had previously been imagined.
- Uncertain what future to strive for after realizing a lack of desire for sex or romance.
- Worry over the kind of family to create in the future, particularly without a long-term romantic partner.
- Worry over being valued by others without the possibility of sex or romance.

"It got me to thinking what might happen if my own parents ever [need full-time care]. I am an only child, I am ace, and while I might someday have a partner it certainly isn't the 1+1= 2 formula that most people seem to expect. Will I be left by myself with two aging parents and nobody around to support me? How will I manage on my own?"—Torie

"Part of me wants a romantic partner to share my life with. Part of me thinks that the concept of dating is plain exhausting. Part of me wants to experience love. Part of me wants to avoid heartbreaks at all cost. Part of me doesn't want to die

alone. Part of me is relieved that I don't fall in love easily. Part of me is scared that, what if I don't fall in love at all? What if I do, the only time I do, the person of interest doesn't feel the same way? I do find people attractive, but I've never liked anyone that way enough to consider wanting to date them. It's quite a mess. Honestly, I don't know what I want."—Rui

The fears about creating a future can be relieved by understanding goals and ideals for the future, making it easier to create a plan. We explore this idea more later in this chapter.

Recontextualizing Past Experiences

Realizing and understanding that one is ace or aro can provide better understandings of past experiences. Past attempts at romantic or sexual relationships, and consequent failures or misunderstandings with partners, can make a lot more sense once the ace or aro person realizes that they do not experience the attraction that many others do in those situations. They may also realize that what they thought was romantic or sexual attraction actually was not.[5] They may miss sexual innuendos, sex jokes, or others' attempts at flirting or wooing. Even non-romantic and non-sexual interactions can make more sense once it becomes clear that others are operating within a paradigm that they are not.

Imagine a hypothetical aro person named Fiero. After they accept their identity, they may realize that some of the social awkwardness they experienced was due to their orientation. For example, their friends Glinda and Nessa seemed to be avoiding each other and blushing when they do see each other. Fiero may eventually realize that they were attracted to each other, and that caused the discomfort. This may seem obvious to most

---

5   See "Attraction Confusion" in Chapter 4.

people, but for many aro and ace people, this kind of social interaction is entirely foreign.

> *"Once I started identifying as asexual, a lot of parts of myself made a lot more sense. I was able to see all the small things from various experiences and situations in my life that all connected to being asexual and that led to me understanding myself and my own needs and wants in a completely new way."—Anonymous*

> *"It's hard to do a good job of reinterpreting the past, but the conclusion I've come to is that feelings for around a dozen people that I thought were crushes were really squishes, more platonic feelings. I was just living in a very heteronormative environment."—Rebecca C*

OUR ADVICE

- Remember that you have more information now than you did in the past, and try to forgive your past self for any mistakes you may have made.
- It's okay to grieve the loss of time and experiences that you might have had if you had realized your aromanticism or asexuality earlier.
- Recontextualizing past experiences can also be painful because it may lead you to uncover ways that you have experienced oppression—both aphobia and other intersecting systems of oppression—that you had not previously been able to articulate. As you work through these experiences, make sure to take care of yourself in any ways that you need.
- The action of recontextualizing your past can provide clarity, which can be empowering! If you don't feel this way right away, that's okay; it may come in time.

- Consider talking to other queer people about this—it is a fairly common experience, particularly for those who realize their identities later in life.

Imagining an Ace/Aro Future

One of the more difficult aspects of accepting an aro or ace identity is picturing a future. From the time they are young, most people have an idea about how their future will look. That idea is usually based on societal norms, which is typically het-ero-, amato-, and allonormative. Most people generally assume that they will form a long-term romantic and sexual relationship, live with their partner, and get married and have children. However, most ace and aro people rethink these assumptions after realizing their identity.

> *"To me being ace and aro means that I don't have to follow some script that others wrote for me, I can just live my life in a way that feels right. I feel validated and empowered by the knowledge that I'm not the only one."*—Anna M

For many ace and aro people, it will be important to seriously consider what kind of long-term relationships they wish to have, if any at all. Societal structures and norms prescribe a very specific relationship structure that includes monogamy, sex, and romance, and it is common for people in the ace and aro communities to find these criteria undesirable. Some ace and aro people may choose to never partner, and others need to figure out the boundaries and desires that will guide their relationships. Since the ace and aro communities are newer than other queer communities, there is very little representation of alternatives to the societally expected relationship model. Therefore, most ace and aro people have to start from scratch, without examples of others like them who have built successful lives for themselves.

Some ace and aro people choose not to pursue partnered relationships. This means they will have to navigate a society that presumes that everyone will end up partnered. It means relying only on yourself for housing, financial support, health-care benefits, emotional support, and housework. While many of these supports can be achieved through non-partnered relationships, they are less likely to be permanent and will not guarantee benefits conferred by law. There is also no inherent expectation that these kinds of support are a part of non-partnered relationships, so they will need to be negotiated on a case-by-case basis. This process is emotionally difficult at best.

Many ace and aro people will go through a stage of grieving for a lost future when they realize their future will not involve such a relationship. Society outlines certain futures for everyone, including dating, cohabitation, marriage, and a nuclear family. This is another example of amatonormativity. Let's say there's a hypothetical aro person named Lee. He may have never thought concretely about his potential future, but the hazy ideas in his mind probably involved living in a home with a significant other and eventually having children. When he realizes that he is aromantic and does not actually want a long-term partner, he may need time to mourn this idea of his future. It is not particularly the loss of the hypothetical spouse that he is mourning but other aspects of that future, such as the ability to afford a house due to dual income or the convenience of having a stable presence to walk his dog.

> "There needs to be greater representation of folks not in monogamous relationships and representation of all the different possibilities there are. I'm kind of just making things up as I go, and I'm pretty sure I'm not thinking of a whole load of possibilities I might want to consider, simply because one brain isn't enough for that."—Anonymous

Deciding the Importance of the Label

Everyone has certain aspects of their identity that are more relevant than others. After adopting an ace or aro identity, each individual will need to decide how that identity flows with their overall sense of self and how large of a role it will play in their life. They will potentially need to decide if their aro or ace identity takes precedence over other romantic or sexual orientations that they hold. Then there is the matter of how important their orientation is in comparison to other identities they might hold, with regards to race, ethnicity, disability, career, socioeconomic class, gender identity, religion, likes and dislikes, political affiliations, and other identities.

Some may find that ace or aro identities have little impact in their day-to-day life. Others may struggle to accept their new labels and feel a sense of reluctance, shame, or disassociation with the label. These are all valid outlooks on a person's aro or ace identity. Not all ace or all aro people will consider that ace or aro identity to be a huge part of their identity and daily life.

Some determine the prevalence of an identity by how much it affects their daily life and personal interactions.

"Being aromantic and asexual means that I cannot draw my lines as cleanly as romantic asexuals or aromantic non-asexuals can. For me, my sexuality is collectively a term used to describe my lack of the attractions that most people naturally possess: sexual and romantic. I tend to relate more toward one half of my identity or the other depending on the social situation I am in at the time, though I mostly identify more with my aromanticism on any given day. My asexuality comes into play when people discuss sexual topics, when I am forced to watch sexual scenes in media, or when people discuss safe sex or childbirth."—Rhys G

"I identify as bisexual as well as asexual. I'm probably technically biromantic, but I identify with the bisexual label more. [...] While learning more about queer theory I began to understand the different types of attraction. And from that I realized that a) I am bisexual because I really am attracted to more than one gender, and b) that I'm asexual because that attraction isn't sexual. Now that I've had time to settle into those identities, I outwardly identify more with the bisexual community than I do the ace community. For me, bisexual equals the who I want to have relationships with, and asexual is the how I want to experience those relationships."—Karin

Some people formulate their identity based on the understanding and expectations of those around them.

"I first came out as bisexual/pansexual and—while I encountered prejudice from classmates/acquaintances—it was more readily accepted by family and friends than asexuality. When I later came out as panromantic asexual, most of my relatives did not believe me because they don't think asexuality is real. They say 'You just haven't met the right person' or 'You shouldn't get a different label from other bisexual people just because you don't want to have a lot of sex with strangers.' (They don't believe that I do not—or will not—ever want sex.) Typically, when coming out to someone who is not a close friend, I simply say 'I'm queer. I don't care about gender and I'm not very sexual' in order to avoid using the labels people outside of the queer community find confusing."—Minerva

Finally, as with any other identity, acceptance and a feeling of compatibility with one's identity as ace or aro takes time to solidify and feel natural. Further, everyone reaches a different point of acceptance and comfort with their identity. These feelings play into how one decides to identify, and how to feel a connection to this identity, and therefore the importance of this identity. However, feelings of discomfort or shame when relating to one's identity do not directly correspond with how strongly a person identifies with it. Strong negative feelings, like strong positive feelings, can indicate how important an identity is.

Negativity Towards Romance or Sex

Ace and aro individuals who have only recently realized that they are influenced by the social norms of compulsory sexuality and amatonormativity will often go through a period of feeling intense negative emotions towards sex and compulsory sexuality, towards romance and amatonormativity, or sometimes towards both. This may lead aro or ace individuals to develop a very judgmental mentality towards the rest of allo society, as well as towards individuals who are romance-favorable and sex-favorable. This may hold particularly true for those who are uninterested in or repulsed by sex or romance but felt burdened by pressure to conform to society's expectations. An ace or aro person may be reacting to the fact that society's ways of treating sex and romance have been hurtful to them and to others.

Aro and ace people can begin to feel negatively about small daily interactions that are representative of amatonormative and allonormative culture. These feelings can include, but are not limited to:

- frustration with wedding planning
- annoyance with romantic storylines in media
- aversion to seeing naked, near-naked, or sexualized bodies
- hatred of public displays of affection
- confusion about sex jokes, euphemisms, and innuendo
- anger at the near-constant questioning of anyone's singleness

- discomfort with sexuality in advertising and media
- horror, disgust, or confusion with strangers flirting with you
- dislike of dating/hook-up culture and things related to it (dating apps, clubs, etc.).

Aromantic and asexual people have every right to feel negatively about interacting with romance or sex. However, personal repulsions can, and should, remain separate from understanding that others have the right to enjoy consensual sex and romance. Being sex- and romance-positive politically and being sex- and romance-repulsed or averse are not mutually exclusive.

Finally, ace or aro community spaces can provide a setting where you can be surrounded by others who feel similarly critical of mainstream narratives about sex or romance. It can be exciting and validating to express pent-up frustrations, fears, and other feelings about sex, romance, or related behaviors. These can also be safe spaces free of any romantic or sexual content or innuendo.

Sciatrix, on her blog *Writing from Factor X*,[6] described this phenomenon in November of 2010 as similar to "detoxing":

I've seen a lot of people go through this phase I think of as detoxing. That is, they're coming out of a culture that expects everyone to want sex, anyone in a romantic relationship to have it, and they find this space that's validating their disinterest in sex or their outright repulsion at the activity. And they're excited, they're relieved, they're integrating this new identity, and they sometimes get pretty enthusiastic about how terrible sex is and how much they hate it, because they've never had anywhere to say that before and

---

6   Sciatrix (2010) "A Response to SlightlyMetaphysical." Accessed on 24/5/2022 at https://writingfromfactorx.wordpress.com/2010/11/29/a-response -to-slightlymetaphysical.

have people nod their heads and say "yeah, I get it, I don't experience that desire to have sex with people either."

What needs to happen in asexual communities is a validation of personal feelings about sex for oneself (that is, if you are repulsed by sex that is okay, and if you love sex to bits that is also okay), while not allowing that detoxing stage to spill over into criticizing other people's choices. (That is, no saying "sex is inherently bad, no one should be having sex, sex should be banned.")

Although Sciatrix here is describing the asexual experience specifically, it applies as much to or more to aromantic people, as it is often much more difficult to avoid romance in the same way as others avoid sex. For example, it is inappropriate to discuss sex in most workplaces, but discussing dating lives is usually encouraged. It is also incredibly challenging to find media to consume without a central romantic plot, while there are many categories of media that make no reference to sex at all.

Similar to what Sciatrix explained for newly identifying aces, individuals new to identifying as aro will often seek safe spaces for validation of their personal feelings about romantic relationships, romantic feelings, and romantic behaviors, and these aro people may be prone to making generalizations that don't apply to all romantic dynamics, such as expressing the idea that romantic relationships are inherently less deep, lasting, or pure than friendships.

An ideal space for an aro or ace individual new to identifying with one of these identities would be one with people who gently react to these natural inclinations to vent and disparage. Ace or aro people with more experience in community spaces can help newer members understand how to differentiate between statements about their own personal experiences and feelings and statements that are hurtful and overly critical of other people's choices and therefore go too far. Some of those statements can even invalidate other ace and aro individuals within their own communities, either within their identity or just around their personal behavior.

For example, take Natty, an aromantic person who loves reading romance novels. They may feel that they have to hide this hobby in aromantic communities, as they are surrounded by people who disparage romance in media. They should be able to express their enjoyment of romance without worry of being mocked, ostracized, or invalidated. However, aromantic people who are romance-repulsed should also be validated, as their negative personal feelings about romance in their own lives may be core to their new identity and something many others share.

OUR ADVICE

- It is okay if you need to vent about and disparage sex and romance generally. Find a safe space to do so or a safe person who will listen.
- Once you get your negative feelings about romance or sex out, reflect on what you expressed. Try to separate your own personal feelings from making judgments about others, and try to remain romance- and sex-positive.
- Reflect on which aspects of sex and romance you may dislike seeing or hearing about. Keep track of the specific experiences you have that provoke negative feelings and see if you can identify any patterns.
- Remember that the forms of romance and sex portrayed in pop culture and elevated by society are not the only forms that exist.
- Seek out other communities who may feel similarly and where you might be able to share your feelings, receive validation, and learn from others.
- Seek out entertainment that avoids romance or sex.

CHAPTER 9

Part Six—Coming Out

Asexuality and Aromanticism Compared with Other LGBTQIA+ Identities

When coming out, ace and aro people may have some of the same experiences as other LGBTQIA+ people. It may be anxiety inducing for anyone to come out, especially when the person has little coming-out experience or when the environment to share this information may be unfriendly. On the other hand, the coming-out experience may be easy and fulfilling, and initiating the conversation may be easy. Reactions to coming out will also differ from confidant to confidant. The experience of everyone who comes out is sure to be different.

There should be no judgment surrounding an individual's decision on whether to come out. While coming out may seem necessary or important in many circles, and not being out can be seen as deceptive, the real problem is that society places the onus on queer people to be open about their identities rather than on everyone else to not be hetero-, amato-, allo-, and cisnormative. As long as you are respecting your own safety, needs, and comfort, any decision you make about coming out is the right one for you.

"My ideal way of coming out is not coming out at all. I know why it's a thing, but I wished that gay, bi, pan, trans, any queer

people didn't have to do this coming out thing. I want being queer to be treated as a normal thing."—Rui

There are many reasons aro and ace people come out to others in their lives. Many of these overlap with the reasons of most other LGBTQIA+ people. Here are some, though not all, of the reasons ace and aro people may choose to come out:

- Their identity or orientation is an important part of their life, who they are, and how they define themselves in the world around them.
- It feels like omitting or avoiding an important part of themselves otherwise.
- It will help set expectations for their future and serious relationships with others.
- It will help them find people to share their life or build a future with.
- It may help them navigate their relationships with other people, no matter how casual the relationship.
- It builds self-esteem.
- It alleviates the stress of hiding their identity.
- It is something they're proud of and they want to share it with others.

Some people may not come out to anyone, because they may see their identity as irrelevant, unimportant, or tangential to their relationships with others and not feel the need to connect to any larger community. This may be particularly true for people who discover labels for their identities late in life. For example, someone who never felt the desire to partner or date and has surrounded themselves with people who support them may find out that there is a label that fits their experience: aromantic. They may recognize it or even start using it in reference to themself, but as the label does not change who they are or their behavior, they may not decide to tell others about this new description.

When deciding whether or how to come out, ace and aro people share certain fears with other queer people, such as:

- fear of being outed in contexts where the person did not want to come out
- fear of violence[1]
- fear of being denied affection.

Unfortunately, for some people, these fears do come to pass. Homophobia, transphobia, and aphobia can be powerful forces that impact how societies treat LGBTQIA+ people.

However, coming out also presents unique concerns to many aro and ace people that other queer people do not experience. The principal difference that an ace or aro person could experience when coming out is based on the ignorance of most people around aro or ace identities. The terminology of ace and aro communities is generally unknown to people outside of the community, whereas some language of other LGBTQIA+ identities has made it into the mainstream (butch, bisexual, pride, etc.). A person may have never heard of ace or aro identities before someone comes out to them. This means that an aro or ace person is likely to experience greater misunderstanding when coming out when compared with people coming out as other identities. Therefore, when ace and aro people do decide to come out for themselves, they often have to provide an explanation for their orientation, community, and their community's culture as a whole.

Since ace and aro orientations are less visible, ace and aro people may feel less of a need or desire to come out as ace or aro. If an ace or aro person identifies as another LGBTQIA+

---

1 More on this in "Violence," later in this chapter.

identity, they may find it easier to prioritize that other identity when coming out because people are more likely to be familiar with that identity. This does not necessarily mean they more strongly identify with that other identity.

An ace or aro person who does not identify with other LGBTQIA+ identities may be perfectly fine with being seen as heterosexual and heteroromantic and feel no desire to come out. However, the opposite may be true: an aro or ace person may be very uncomfortable and unhappy with feeling unable to come out as the identity that is more important and relevant to them.

Aro and ace people may, on average, come out later in life than people of other LGBTQIA+ identities, particularly because, as explained in Chapter 4, the relative obscurity of aro and ace identities makes it hard to recognize them as legitimate possibilities. Some ace and aro people do figure out their orientation fairly early in life, and some people of other queer orientations discover these identities later in life, so no one narrative or timeline can capture the realization and coming-out experience for everyone of one identity. There are, however, some common issues and fears with regards to coming out that we'll explore in the next section.

Common Issues and Fears

Coming out can be difficult regardless of identity. However, ace and aro people in particular face a lot of unique challenges when coming out, in addition to the common issues one would expect across all identities. Here, we will discuss some of the specific issues that may prevent you from feeling fully comfortable coming out or may worsen the coming-out experience. Fear of coming out can be intensified if someone you've come out to has already reacted negatively. If you're coming out, you are the best judge of how likely a given outcome is in your specific circumstance.

The Ace or Aro 101 Talk

Ace and aro identities are often not well known by the general public, so it can be very hard to predict how familiar any particular person is with aro or ace identities. An ace or aro person coming out may be someone else's first exposure to those orientations. Naturally, this can lead to a lot of questions, including very personal or invasive questions. This can put the ace or aro person in a position where they feel like they have to answer everything, from an introduction to the identity itself, to an in-depth explanation of their own feelings, before they can be taken seriously.

> *"I feel like I can never come out without a 20-point slideshow and a full explanation. It gets tiring, especially when by the end of it they will sometimes not be accepting."*—Alyssa

The process of having to explain the details of an identity can be exhausting, especially if it becomes a regular occurrence. There is also the concern that the ace or aro person may not have all the answers for the questions being asked. Being questioned on the legitimacy of one's own identity can feel like a personal attack. What is true for one aro or ace person is not necessarily true for the community in general, and the aro or ace person may feel torn between representing their own experience and representing the community's diversity. Some ace or aro people decide that it's not worth the trouble of having to explain themselves and decide instead to stay closeted.

It can also be more difficult to come out as ace or aro because you may feel a responsibility to educate others about the whole community rather than just defining your own identity and experiences. A demiromantic person explaining their orientation should not have to also explain the entire aromantic spectrum, as well as the SAM and asexuality, but because they do not want to leave others with incorrect ideas about their community, they may feel obliged to do so anyway. In addition, educating others about identities that you do not have when you have not learned how to do so can be harmful, as you may accidentally spread misconceptions. A relevant analogy would be asking Yolanda, a binary trans person, to explain being nonbinary—it's not an identity that she holds, she should not have to represent all non-cis individuals, and nonbinary people should get to share their own experiences.

Also, some identities even within aro and ace communities are lesser known, understood, and respected, and coming out as one of those identities can be more daunting because of the stigmas attached. These identities may also require greater nuance and knowledge than a 101 usually covers. Later in this chapter, we will cover some of the differences in coming out as various ace and aro identities.

> *"I do wish people would ask more questions, because I know nobody really knows anything beyond the absolute basics, and I'd rather they ask me than someone else. I don't really mind talking about it. But I don't think they know what questions to even ask. They don't want to step on a landmine or something. But that means they go forward with no understanding at all. The 'leaving it unspoken' thing drives me crazy."—Kathryn S*

OUR ADVICE

- Know that when you come out, you do not owe any-one any answers about your identities or experiences.
- Have go-to resources you can share with others when you come out to them instead of having to explain your identities yourself (including this book!).[2]

---

2   See the Appendix for some resources.

- Remember that you don't have to explain any of the nuances of your identity.
- When you come out, keep in mind that you don't have to represent anyone other than yourself.
- If the pressure of educating others is hindering you from coming out when you do want to come out otherwise, focus on your main goal. Think about what you hope to achieve by coming out, and don't get too distracted by the 101 talk.
- If explaining the details of asexuality or aromanticism might provoke the person to whom you are coming out to threaten your safety, you do not need to use this approach.

Coming Out Again

It is fairly common for someone to have already come out as some other queer identity before coming out as ace or aro. This can be either because they have some other LGBTQIA+ identity or because during the questioning process they mistook their specific ace or aro spectrum identity for either another queer identity or for another aro or ace identity. They might have difficulty coming out again because:

- they feel like they're "betraying" a former identity or community or may worry they will lose community, friends, or support after coming out again
- they're tired of doing the work of coming out and explaining their identities to others
- they worry that others may not accept their new identity or may see it as another "phase"
- if both the previous identity and the current identity are true at once, they might not know how to explain the nuances of their identities combined

- they may not know how to explain that their identity shifted and they no longer identify in the same way
- they may not be believed or trusted to know themselves when they tell someone they were wrong about their previous identity
- they may worry that "adding" extra orientations will lead to confusion and backlash or that they will reach a breaking point of acceptance
- they may think that other people get tired of their identity exploration
- they might feel the need to justify past behaviors
- they worry that people may see their new identity as in conflict with another identity they hold.

It may be easier for the ace or aro person to not disclose their ace or aro identity to save themselves from the issues of clarifying how they changed or added identities.

> "I think my biggest hesitancy was that I had previously come out as gay to a number of friends and family, so had to deal with the confusion and questions associated with changing labels. There also were a number of friends in my life who I had previously lied to and made up romantic or sexual experiences. It was hard for me to tell people I had lied to them because I had been ashamed of the way I am."—Nicole G

OUR ADVICE

- Again, remember that you don't owe anyone anything when coming out.
- Know that the experience of coming out multiple times is exceedingly common in the ace and aro communities. Seek out narratives of other aro and ace people who have come out multiple times.

- Weigh the pros and cons of coming out, and consider how much energy and time you are willing to give people in your life.
- Be aware of potential safety and security concerns with coming out. If you have these concerns and still want to come out, come up with a safety plan.
- If you are concerned you may lose your current community, make a plan for finding new communities, or make sure you have some community spaces you won't lose by learning more about the community's understanding and acceptance of aro and ace people. You may want to seek out communities of aro and ace people who also share other identities that you hold.

Distinctions in Coming Out as Various Ace and Aro Identities

Aro and ace identities are not a monolith—there are many individual identities within these spectrums that are even less known than asexuality or aromanticism. Many of these identities come with extra complications when coming out. Because of the number of different identities, we cannot describe all of the individual difficulties associated with each, so we will focus on some of the most common themes.

VARIORIENTED SEXUAL AND ROMANTIC ORIENTATIONS

Sometimes orientations match—for example, someone who is both aromantic and asexual or someone who is both panromantic and pansexual. Sometimes a person's orientations don't match each other. For people whose romantic, sexual, or other orientations do not match, it can be frustrating to explain them separately, as it almost means coming out multiple times at once. Both alloace and alloaro fall into this category.

It is also a common assumption that certain orientations are exclusive of others. People may believe that being bi prevents you from being a lesbian or that being ace prevents you from being gay. The person trying to come out with varioriented orientations may run into these assumptions, and the people they're coming out to may try to coerce them into only using one orientation label and invalidate or insult them for thinking that they can use more than one orientation label.

ALLOARO

Since aromanticism is so often seen as a subset of or equivalent to asexuality, coming out as aromantic and allosexual is often met with confusion or disbelief. Along with that, allosexual aromantic people are often saddled with stereotypes about being promiscuous, lacking any emotional connection to others, or even being predatory.

ALLOACE

There is an assumption that one of the ultimate expressions of romantic love is sex and that if someone is in a romantic relationship without sex or without sexual attraction, their love is somehow worth less or inadequate. This assumption is perpetuated in many different areas of society, including in some marriage laws, where marriages aren't finalized unless they are "consummated" through sex. It can be particularly difficult to come out to people as ace when others might automatically assume that they are therefore uninterested in a romantic relationship.

GRAYROMANTIC OR GRAYSEXUAL

Both as umbrella labels and as labels in themselves, grayromanticism and graysexuality are often dismissed or misunderstood identities. While we consider anyone who chooses to identify as ace or aro, including grayromantic or graysexual people, as part of the ace or aro communities, others both in and outside the aro and ace communities may not agree that they "count." It can also be difficult to explain how someone's individual and subjective attractions are different from alloromantic or allosexual attractions. An onus may be placed on grayromantic and graysexual people to prove that they are "gray enough," though the audience may never understand the spectrum of aro and ace identities.

MICROLABELS

Many people who identify strongly with specific microlabels will be seen as "trying to be special."[3] Even without that stumbling block, it can be difficult to explain the details of an ultra-specific, often unseen identity to even the most willing audience. Some people may lose interest or may not consider the nuances of the identity important, feeling they only need to grasp the broad strokes, while the ace or aro person in question may consider their specific identity incredibly important to understand.

NOT IDENTIFYING WITH A SEXUAL OR ROMANTIC ORIENTATION

While many ace people have a specific romantic orientation, and many aro people have a specific sexual orientation, some aro and ace people do not have any other orientation at all. Some may feel one label covers their identity, in the same way that most straight, gay, and bi people only use one orientation label. Others may disconnect entirely with the concept of a sexual or romantic orientation. Still, there is often an assumption that all ace or aro people must have both sexual and romantic orientations. For example, if an ace person is coming out as ace, they may be worried that they will be asked about their romantic orientation as well, and they may not have an answer, may not be willing to answer, or may answer in a way that does not satisfy their audience.

---

3   For more, see "Thinking Identities are All or Nothing" in Chapter 6.

OUR ADVICE

- Know that there are no rules or requirements about the words you use or don't use to define your identity.
- Look for informational resources that are specific to your identity, including any microlabels you identify as. Keep these resources ready to share with others when you come out so you do not feel the burden or responsibility of educating them.
- Practice a coming-out speech, and if you are comfortable doing so, address some of the most common questions or concerns from other people.
- Educating others about your identity is emotional labor that you do not owe others. If you are uncomfortable answering extensive questions from others when you are trying to come out, remember that you have the right to come out with as little or as much detail as you feel most comfortable with.

Rejection

Rejection can be an awful experience, even traumatic or devastating, for aro and ace people. A person might reject an ace or aro person based on a preconceived worldview. This worldview can include, but is not limited to, religious or political beliefs, a conviction that romantic or sexual relationships are a foundation of the human experience, or a belief in negative ace or aro stereotypes. A person might rationalize their reasons for rejecting a loved one who just came out and might ignore the physical and emotional harm this can cause their loved one, as with other LGBTQIA+ coming-out experiences.

INVALIDATION

All forms of invalidation are a form of rejection, even if it seems extremely minor. Many forms of rejection also involve some inherent invalidation. There are three main types of invalidation: considering the orientation not real or legitimate, thinking of the orientation as an insignificant part of one's life, or dehumanizing a person because of their orientation. Dehumanizing itself can come in many forms, from literally calling someone non-human by calling them a plant, robot, or monster for their orientation, to thinking of them as incomplete without romantic or sexual partners or experiences.

Some forms of invalidation can be more harmful based on other intersecting identities. For example, someone younger may have more difficulty being invalidated with jokes, as they may be used to not being taken seriously. On the other hand, people of color are and have historically been dehumanized with comparisons to animals or other non-human entities, so being called a monster may impact them more severely.

Some invalidating statements and actions come from the person not knowing enough about the identity to realize that what they've said can be hurtful. Some invalidation may be based around the assumption that someone coming out does not know themselves or their identity well enough to identify a certain way. Some invalidation, however, might be purposefully hurtful. All forms of invalidation can cause significant distress or harm.

Amatonormativity, heteronormativity, and compulsory sexuality all contribute to the ways and reasons that people invalidate aro and ace identities. Whatever the reason, it can be extremely damaging to the ace or aro person, especially if they are doubting their orientation themselves or if they are coming out to someone they hold in high regard.

> *"After confiding in a close friend I thought that I could trust only to be told that I was wrong, and that sexual activity was the only way to 'correct' that, I began to despise myself. Why couldn't I be normal?"—Az*

Invalidating statements are, unfortunately, so common that they are a frequent discussion topic in ace and aro communities.[4] As a humorous way of coping with these statements and bonding with others in the communities, we created bingo cards for invalidating statements said to aro and ace people; you can find the cards in the appendix.

> *"When you come out as ace, people tend to not believe you, they think that you are wrong, that they know better than you. Most of that is due to ignorance, most people are well meaning, I have no problem with questions, but people shouldn't act like they know how I feel more than I do."*—Matt S

FORMS OF REJECTION

There are types of rejection that have higher stakes than invalidation alone. These types of rejection are rooted in threats to someone's physical, social, or mental safety or wellbeing. Some forms of rejection only tend to occur within certain types of relationships; those specifics will be addressed later in this chapter. As is the case with invalidation, other forms of rejection can be more harmful based on other intersecting identities. For example, being financially cut off may be more harmful for someone whose identities make it harder for them to find stable employment, based on biases around education, disability, race, or other identities.

These types of rejection include:

- the identity being unacknowledged, dismissed, or forgotten
- being financially cut off
- losing housing

---

4   Some of these statements are discussed in greater detail in Chapter 2.

- being pathologized or forced into corrective therapy or another medical treatment[5]
- social isolation or being prevented from seeing friends or a partner
- deprivation of the internet
- being accused of lying previously during past romantic or sexual interactions
- risk of a breakup
- risk of physical, emotional, or sexual trauma or violence, including sexual or romantic coercion[6]
- misguided advice
- withholding of necessary medical or therapeutic treatment
- having family, friends, or partners withhold or be reluctant to show affection or intimacy
- another person expressing disappointment or pressure related to an assumed future that lacks a wedding or offspring
- another person dismissing negative experiences, particularly compared with other orientations
- being judged or pitied for the potential or assumed self-deprivation of sex, romance, or partners
- dehumanizing statements
- being left out of conversations because an aro or ace point of view is seen as invalid
- being rejected sexually or romantically because of assumptions about asexuality or aromanticism.

Any of these forms of rejection can cause emotional harm for the person being rejected. This can damage one's self-esteem

---

5   More on this in "Violence" later in this chapter.
6   More on this in "Violence" later in this chapter.

and cause shame, loneliness, and sadness. It can also tempo-
rarily or permanently damage a relationship.

> *"I don't think my family really understands what it means to*
> *be Aro, and I think a part of them are grieving the experiences*
> *they won't see me have. I haven't been cast out, and they don't*
> *treat me any differently. Still...sometimes I wish I could lean*
> *on them a little more."—Kalinda*

OUR ADVICE

- Always remember that your identities *are* valid, and so
  are you.
- Even if it is hard to remember in the moment, know
  that another person's first reactions may not necessarily reflect their overall opinion, and they might react
  better after thinking things through.
- Give yourself permission to be angry at others for not
  reacting well.
- Prepare resources that you can give to other people so
  that you do not have to educate them yourself. While
  it is not your responsibility to educate them at all,
  having these resources ready in advance can make it
  easier for you in the moment if you choose to do so.
- If you do not want to educate others for any reason,
  that is okay! It is not your responsibility to "fix" others'
  reactions or educate them.
- Look at the bingo cards in the Appendix to remind
  yourself that you are in good company.
- Prepare responses to some of the most frequent kinds
  of invalidating comments so that you know what to do
  if someone says something invalidating to you. Your
  responses can take the form of education, expressing
  feelings, setting boundaries, or something else.

- Remember that you can choose to disengage with people who invalidate you. You are not in control of others' reactions but that does not mean you have to continue subjecting yourself to them.
- Reflect on the different kinds of invalidation listed above and consider whether any are particular fears or triggers for you. If any stand out, try to figure out the likelihood of that rejection happening and make a safety plan.
- While self-expression may be a meaningful goal for you, it is important to prioritize your safety, housing, and financial security. You do not owe your identity to anyone, particularly when your safety is threatened.

Violence

In some circumstances, an ace or aro person may face violence after disclosing their ace or aro identity. Several of the forms of rejection listed above are forms of violence. All of the forms of violence listed here can also be considered forms of rejection. Although some violent acts listed here are extreme, they have been experienced by people who have come out. Many forms of violence overlap with the kinds of violence that other LGBTQIA+ people face. However, other forms of violence are unique to aro and ace people. Some ace and aro people have boundaries that allo people have never considered possible. Allo people may invalidate or minimize, or they may dismiss these boundaries because of general invalidation of the ace or aro person's entire orientation.

No form of violence exists in a vacuum. When there is a greater power imbalance, the risk of violence is higher. Aces and aros who have multiple marginalized identities may be at greater risk of violence and abuse because of the greater disparities in power and privilege. While we separate these forms of violence into different categories, there is a lot of overlap between violent actions and the harm they cause. Examples from all of these types of violence can occur in person and online.

- Verbal abuse can include the use of terms and phrases like "heartless," "robot," "plant," and "uptight" to alienate or hurt ace and aro people; bullying and harassment can be examples of verbal abuse.
- Psychological abuse involves invalidating, gaslight-ing, and other ways of interfering with an aro or ace person's perception of reality or ability to trust themselves.
- Emotional abuse can be actions such as shaming someone for their orientation, guilt-tripping them, or targeting their self-esteem. It heavily overlaps with other kinds of abuse, including verbal abuse and psychological abuse.
- Sexual violence includes sexual harassment, rape, and sexual assault; what constitutes these nonconsensual actions varies from person to person depending on their individual boundaries around sex and sexual content.
- Romantic violence includes non-consensual romantic actions (including what is said) towards someone else; much like sexual actions can be violating, romantic actions can be violating too.
- Spiritual violence involves using religion or spirituality to convince someone that their identity is antithetical to a religious ideology, not approved of by a deity or higher power, or shameful to a religious community.
- Pathologization occurs when anyone suggests or insists one's orientation is actually a medical or psy-chological condition
- Medical trauma can occur when a medical professional

imposes some kind of medical intervention on someone against their wishes or coerces them into participating in some kind of treatment, where the "treatment" in question is trying to "cure" their orientation. This can also include tests or psychological screening, as that presents the assumption that there are certain circumstances in which aro and ace identities would not be valid.

- Coercion often occurs in the context of compulsory sexuality and amatonormativity and can occur without either party necessarily realizing just how coercive the situation is. Coercion can be a part of many of these types of abuse.

"The people I choose not to disclose my identity [to] are the ones I know will rebuke me for daring to identify as anything but straight. People can be dangerous no matter how you identify, but identifying as something that is not definitively straight can put you in even more danger. People don't like it when you say you don't feel attraction. They don't believe you. They say you're lying. They get mad because they want you. I may be proud of my identity, but I'm also not going to put myself in a precarious position."—Komi

OUR ADVICE

- If you fear any kind of violence, you do not have to come out.
- Carefully reflect on your personal situation in order to determine how likely your fears are to come true.
- Make a pros and cons list for coming out. As you make your list, keep in mind that there are some cons (like a high risk of violence) that cancel out any and all pros.
- Remember that coming out isn't "all or nothing." If you

need to stay closeted around one or more people in your life because of a high risk of violence, consider whether you may have other individuals it would be safe to come out to in other areas of your life.

- Set boundaries. Think about what boundaries you need or want to draw, decide how you will communicate these boundaries if needed, and create an action plan for what you will do if these boundaries are violated.
- If you are at risk of experiencing violence, work on building a stable support network and creating an exit plan. You do not need to do this alone; you can reach out to others in your life (supportive friends or family members, trusted professionals, or organizations) to help you.
- If needed, seek out resources specific to ace or aro survivors of violence. Be forewarned that many sexual, relationship, or spiritual violence resources may not take into account nuances common to ace and aro identities. Due to a lack of specifically ace or aro resources, it may be necessary to utilize more general resources. Refer to the resources in the Appendix.

Aro and ace individuals may be at an unusually high risk for facing forced medical intervention; to that end, here is some specific advice about that. The reason for this increased risk stems from the existence of medical conditions that may manifest in behaviors that appear like aromanticism or asexuality, such as being disinterested in sex or not wanting to form or sustain romantic connections. There are also some medications and physical health conditions that can cause a decrease in sex drive. For some allo people, giving diagnoses or changing medication would be appropriate, but the diagnosing medical professional has the responsibility of separating out medical conditions from valid identities.

> *"My healthcare professionals always think there's something 'wrong' with me (hormone levels, thyroid, being on SSRIs, etc.) because I don't have a libido or experience sexual attraction. It really feels invalidating because there's nothing wrong with me: it's just how I am and how I'll always be. They want to try other anti-anxiety/depression meds, they want to test my thyroid and I get blood test after blood test, despite me telling them NOTHING IS WRONG! ... It feels awful and embarrassing."—Anonymous*

Even though the DSM-5 creates an exception for those who identify as asexual, many health professionals are not aware of that exception; additionally, if an ace person is not aware of the language around asexuality, they will be falsely pathologized. The DSM-5 does not acknowledge aromanticism at all, and aro people may be at risk of being diagnosed with a personality disorder, post-traumatic stress disorder (PTSD), or an attachment disorder.

> *"Before I identified as aroace, I was seeing a therapist and she was very pushy about me being single. She seemed to think a lot of my problems stemmed from being single and would give me 'homework' to go out to bars and meet men. I would tell her that I was happy being single and she would insist. It was very unpleasant."—Kara*

OUR ADVICE

- Look for the following qualities in your health professional:

- Someone who does not pathologize your identity and works to gain your trust.
- Someone who advertises themself on lists of LGBTQIA+-friendly health professionals and actively demonstrates their support for the community.
- Someone who focuses on things that are stressors and that you are specifically seeking treatment for rather than "treating" traits that are not causing you distress.
- If you feel comfortable coming out to your doctor, they should validate you and demonstrate that they believe you.
- If you have experienced prior trauma connected to medical interventions in the past and are comfortable sharing that with your doctor, they should believe you, take your experiences seriously, and work to find treatments that will undo or lessen those harms.

• If you are struggling to find a doctor who you are confident has some or all of these qualities, ask for help from other aro or ace people, other LGBTQIA+ people, or local aro, ace, or LGBTQIA+ organizations.

• If someone suggests that you need treatment for your identity, do not believe them. There is a difference between treating your identity and treating stressors that are related to your identity.

• If you are underage, you still have the right to refuse treatment or demand the correct treatment.

• If your identity has both medical and non-medical causes, do not feel guilt or shame about seeking medical care.

The People Ace and Aro Individuals Come Out To

Although the above fears can apply when coming out to anyone, ace and aro people may also have specific concerns when coming out to particular people or within the context of particular relationships.

Partners

Ace and aro people almost always feel they have to come out to current or potential partners. However, this is not true—partners do not deserve to have every piece of information, and that includes identities.

Even if a person doesn't prioritize their ace or aro identity, they will likely need to set boundaries in partnered or intimate relationships as a direct result of their identity. For example, an ace person might want to explain to their romantic partner(s) that they don't want sex and why. Another example would be an aro person who might want to let their sexual partner(s) know that they don't want to go on romantic dates, whatever that may entail. Of course, these are just two examples; both aro and ace people may want to or choose to engage in partnered relationships with varying elements of romance, sex, or both, and that can vary depending on their partner, specific orientation(s), or comfort level with romance or sex.

Some people discover they are ace or aro while they are already in a partnership. Aro or ace people may also wait to see if the relationship has a chance to become long term or serious before divulging this information, especially if they are uncertain about their partner's views on aromanticism or asexuality, though this can come with its own risk of being accused of withholding information.

This conversation can be particularly tricky to navigate, as it often means a restructuring of the relationship. Further, there is the real fear that their partner will feel like the restructuring will be limiting the relationship in a way that won't be easy or possible to accept in order to maintain the relationship. Consider these hypothetical partnerships:

- Akhmed is coming out to his husband Barrold as asexual, and because of his orientation, he specifically wishes to stop having sex. Barrold might feel personally rejected since he, as an allosexual person, might not understand a lack of interest in sex and may interpret it in a way that assumes that Akhmed finds Barrold unattractive or undesirable.
- Carla is coming out to her girlfriend Destiny as aromantic. Destiny might worry that Carla has just fallen out of love with her or become bored with their romantic activities.

Both Barrold and Destiny also might feel betrayed, thinking that their partners have been lying to them for their entire relationship, even if Akhmed and Carla genuinely didn't know they were ace or aro, respectively. In these cases, the relationships might end, particularly since Akhmed and Carla are sex- and romance-repulsed. Barrold and Destiny, on the other hand, may not want to change their relationships in ways that would accommodate Akhmed's and Carla's needs. This potential fallout can make the decision to come out particularly difficult, as Akhmed and Carla value their relationships and may not want them to end. Furthermore, as in any relationship, there are often practical or emotional ties, such as cohabitation, coparenting (pets or children), shared finances, or shared family or friends, that make dissolving the partnership logistically and emotionally burdensome.

Mixed-orientation relationships are possible and can thrive. Coming out as aro or ace doesn't mean the relationship is necessarily over. However, it takes work to navigate the new understandings of each partner's needs.

> *"I came out [as asexual] to my husband—who obviously deserved to know. It was a little delicate for a week after, and then we both realized that we were still the same people we'd always been and we relaxed into it. It's made everything more relaxed between us."—Marnie*

An additional threat that ace or aro people who are in intimate or partnered relationships face when coming out is being at risk of rape or sexual assault. When an aro or ace person comes out to their partner(s), they often establish their boundaries around sexual activity. Their partner(s) may not respect or take those newly established boundaries seriously, they may feel entitled to sex, or they may not think that consent is necessary. They might sexually violate their partner by pressuring them, guilting them, manipulating them, or physically forcing them into sex. They may also suggest that an aro or ace orientation is not legitimate or that having sex will "fix" their orientation (i.e. corrective rape).

Similarly, aro or ace people may establish boundaries around romantic activities. Because society assumes that consent around romance is always given, these boundaries may be even less likely to be respected than boundaries around sexuality. Partners may violate those boundaries by insisting that their relationship or specific activities are romantic, using pet names or labels with romantic connotations such as "babe" or "boy-friend," demanding specific romantic behavior, or expressing romantic feelings. They may even assert that an activity, or the relationship as a whole, is romantic in a way that invalidates their partners' orientation(s). While most of those romantic actions seem like a given in many partnered or intimate rela-tionships, they can violate the boundaries of some aro and ace people.

In some cases, an ace or aro person will come out to poten-tial partners up front or in the early stages of a relationship.

This can turn away some potential partners, and some aro or ace people will wait to come out until they've established some level of intimacy, hoping by then their partner will be less likely to leave. On the other hand, that requires an emotional investment that could cause them extra pain if the relationship ends because they came out.

> *"I did not mention this experience to anyone for a long time because I was in a relationship, and I didn't want my boyfriend to find out. (I thought he would break up with me if he found out I didn't want to have sex, even after marriage.)"*—Becca

OUR ADVICE

- If you discover your aro or ace identity while you are in a relationship, make a pros and cons list for coming out to your partner(s).
- Remember that you do not have to come out to your partner(s). If you do not feel comfortable coming out to your partner(s), you may want to evaluate the reasons behind that feeling.
- You do not need permission to end your relationship if that seems best.
- If you choose to end your relationship, you can do so without coming out if you do not want to come out.
- On the other hand, you do not necessarily need to end your relationship because of your new-found identity or your recent decision to come out. Your partner(s) may embrace your identity!
- Practice coming out to your partner(s). Predict possible reactions and consider how you might respond. Make a safety plan if needed.
- Work on defining your boundaries and desires in a relationship—one way could be by creating a "Will,

Want, Won't List." There is an example of this in the appendix.

- You and your partner(s) may want to start seeing a couples counselor. Many couples choose to do so; seeing a counselor shows that both parties desire to try to make the relationship work and does not necessarily mean that your relationship is over or should not continue. If you would like to start seeing a couples counselor, see if you can find one competent in aro and ace issues. You can seek recommendations from your local ace or aro community or LGBTQIA+ organizations.
- Consider gathering resources that would help your partner(s) learn about ace or aro identities.

Parents and Other Family

Another common group of people to whom ace and aro people come out is parents and family members. Aro and ace people might come out to their family because they want to explain their lack of interest in certain types of relationships or activities or because they want their family to know them better.

However, many aro and ace people may choose to never come out to family members. This can be in part because it would be risky due to conservative or repressive views of family members, but it also may be because their orientation is irrelevant to their relationship with their family. For instance, an asexual lesbian who is open with her family may choose to come out as a lesbian so that she can talk openly about who she is dating and bring partners to meet her parents, but as her asexuality does not impact her visible romantic life, she may see it as a personal part of her relationship with girlfriends or partners. An aromantic person, on the other hand, may never engage in a romantic relationship, and as that lack of romantic partners can be explained by simply being single, they may choose to avoid having to explain their orientation to their family and engage in a potentially awkward conversation.

Coming out to family members often means informing them that their vision of someone's future was incorrect. Often, family members assume that every generation will want the same amatonormative, heteronormative things the generation before wanted, usually meaning a monogamous marriage and children. Additionally, older family members are less likely to have encountered asexuality or aromanticism as topics, which typically adds to the confusion.

Even the most well-meaning family may accidentally say invalidating statements that undermine ace and aro people's sense of themselves by saying things like "You're just a late bloomer" or "It's just a phase." This can be particularly common with older family members, who may be used to thinking of the aro or ace individual as a child and therefore not old enough to engage in romantic or sexual feelings or actions. An older family member's perspective may be more valued by the ace or aro individual as well, as they are usually seen as wise and authoritative. The family member may also be upset that their child or relative is too "immature" or "rebellious" to engage in sex or romance, as they may feel that romantic and sexual relationships, and the often-presumed marriage and children that will follow, are necessary parts of a successful life. Aromantic people particularly may have to work to convince their parents that this doesn't mean they'll die alone or that they won't have love in their lives, as society tends to place the romantic and sexual relationships above all other kinds of relationships or all kinds of joy.

Parental figures or other family members may demand that the aro or ace person develops romantic relationships or produces children, which they may not want for themselves. The ace or aro person who is being told they are the cause of such disappointment for a loved one may feel doubt about their own desires or pressured to try to change their desires.

Feeling stuck between changing who they are or being rejected by a loved one can result in feeling isolated and unworthy. This rejection may cause isolation or force the ace or aro person to pursue this future apart from their family, even to their own personal detriment.

> *"I am not out as ace to my family, unfortunately, but they are conservative and most of them do not think positively about LGBT+ folks at all. For this reason, we aren't particularly close, and being out to them isn't important to my daily life."—Miranda B*

OUR ADVICE

- Remember that you do not owe your family any details about your lives or orientations, and you do not have to come out to your family, even if you are out to other people in your life.
- Do not feel obligated to have certain relationships because your family expects or wants you to.
- Make a pros and cons list about coming out to your family. Consider possible reactions that they may have and how you will respond in those scenarios. Make a safety plan if needed.
- As you are exploring whether to come out to your family, you may consider coming out to certain family members but not others. If you are thinking about this option, keep in mind that your relatives may inform each other, even unintentionally. This is especially relevant with younger relatives who may be unable to keep secrets or relatives who live together.
- If you choose to come out to your family, make a plan for how and when you will come out. Practice what you will tell them.

- Gather educational resources to give to family members so that you are not responsible for explaining your identity. It may be particularly helpful for families to have these resources because they can take some of the emotion out of the learning process.
- Develop a found family through friends, particularly other queer friends, whether or not you come out to your family, but especially if your family seems likely to exhibit a negative reaction to your identity.
- You can and should feel free to cut ties with family members who do not respect your orientation(s). If you do not want to cut ties completely, you can set other boundaries with your family.

Medical Professionals
DOCTORS

Many asexual people who come out to their doctor do so when asked whether they are sexually active, a standard question in a physical and history exam. It is also common for ace people to feel extremely uncomfortable when asked about their "sex life" or "sexual activity," whether from societally induced shame or sexual repulsion. Sometimes doctors might assume a history or experience of trauma when their patient is an adult who is not sexually active. Doctors may also say invalidating statements that imply that the person should become sexually active soon or will definitely be sexually active at some point. They may also simply disbelieve that their patient is not sexually active.

Coming out can stop doctors from thinking that there is trauma, low libido, or some other health issue that needs to be dealt with. However, if the doctor does not believe that someone is happy being sexually inactive or that asexuality is a real orientation, they may still recommend that their patient undergo tests or trials of medications, which is even more invalidating.

Aromantic people may be asked by doctors or forms if they are married or have a partner and may feel uncomfortable coming out. This is not equivalent to the question of sexual activity, as medical professionals are unlikely to assume an underlying health problem based on marital or partnered status. However, unfortunately, doctors may encourage aros to seek psychiatric help if they do come out.

> *"I haven't come out to healthcare professionals because I am worried it will affect their medical advice. This has caused some issues as I take the pill to regulate my periods and had trouble finding one that suited me. Despite repeatedly emphasizing that I did not need it as a contraceptive, doctors kept prescribing me higher dosage pills, making comments such as 'You might as well be safe.' They seemed to generally assume that every woman wants to have sex with someone of the opposite sex. I eventually found the right pill by asking one of my close friends who is a doctor and knows I am asexual."—Anonymous*

MENTAL HEALTHCARE WORKERS

Ace and aro people come out to therapists either while in the process of discovering their identity or when secure in their identity. Aro and ace people may be talking about their identity in the way many people may mention their occupation when speaking to a therapist: as a relevant part of their day-to-day life. Ace and aro people may also be trying to figure out their identities for the first time, and if the therapist doesn't know much about the identities, their attempts to help may do more harm than good. In any case, therapists may want to discover an "underlying cause," which assumes that being aro or ace is a problem that needs to be solved. While ace and aro identities can have a cause, that cause is irrelevant to how the person is currently identifying and often will not be helpful for them to discuss. Choosing to discuss that underlying cause should be up to and led by the patient and not forced into the discussion by the provider, and it is important to validate their orientation no matter the cause or lack thereof.

> *"I also have come out to my therapist but she thinks that my asexuality may be related to my low self-esteem and depression. I don't think that she's right but I can't afford to change therapists. It made me feel invalidated."*—Destiny

Even if they are supportive, therapists are extremely unlikely to know much about asexuality or aromanticism. This means that sessions may involve the patient educating their therapist on the basics of their identity rather than the therapist helping the client to understand or address the deeper nuances that the patient would prefer to discuss.

> *"Talking to mental health professionals, I've found them to be unaware of asexuality, skeptical about it as a thing that exists, and wanting to hear about it from me rather than educate themselves."*—Ari

OUR ADVICE

- Refer back to the "Our Advice" list in the section on violence earlier in this chapter.
- Consider gathering resources to give to your medical professional. If you have access to resources that have a scientific or academic basis, these may be more effective when advocating for yourself in a medical setting.
- Brainstorm possible forms of invalidation you may receive from your medical professional if you come out to them and visualize in advance how you would respond.

- Know that self-advocacy in a medical setting is not easy, and coming out to your medical professional may not have the desired outcome. If that happens, it is not your fault.
- If you have a history of medical trauma or a greater risk of experiencing medical trauma, keep these experiences in mind as you consider whether to come out to your medical professional.
- Consider not coming out with a specific identity at all, but rather just describing your experiences, if you think that this might be more helpful.

Friends

Sexual and romantic orientation can have a large impact on a person's life and, as such, aromantic and asexual people often want to be able to share this with friends who are close to them. Coming out to friends may be especially important for those who are not close to their families and consider their friends to be family or more important than family. People may come out if they wish to give context to how they navigate things such as romance, relationships, sex, and attraction. They also may come out to friends because they want to change or redefine the relationship that already exists. Coming out can give context to this type of change or redefinition. This decision is also often affected by their allo friends' romantic and sexual activity and enthusiasm to discuss it.

Some people may choose to come out because they are tired of being seen as allosexual or alloromantic and want to establish boundaries with their friends. Aromantic people, particularly, often feel left out by their friends when they suggest "couples' nights" or are always focused on their romantic lives. Some aromantic people, and to a lesser degree asexual people, may have to deal with friends trying to set them up on dates or continuously asking about their dating life. For ace people specifically, this can also take the form of setting them up for sexual encounters. A focus on romance, especially over a long period, may hurt friendships, especially if the person is also romance-repulsed. Aromantic people may also have to deal with judgment from their friends if they pursue sexual relationships, as sexual interaction without romantic ties is often considered taboo, promiscuous, or inferior. Asexual people may have to hear discussions about their friends' sex lives, or even may be asked about their own sex lives, and thus may want to come out to set boundaries around how their friends discuss sex around them, based on their personal level of comfort with these kinds of conversations. Friends may be judgmental if there is one person in the group who is not sexually active, not expressing the same sexual interests, or seems disinterested, labeling them as childish, prudish, or sex-negative, or excluding them from certain group activities.

Some ace and aro people may choose to not come out and simply withhold information about that part of their lives. This may be because of any of the fears discussed earlier in this section or because their orientation(s) simply do not impact their relationships with their friends to a meaningful enough degree. They also may worry that their friend will not be able to see them in the same way and that it will significantly change the way their friend treats them as well as the type of relationship they have. However, not coming out can feel inauthentic, as society often assumes by default that people are straight, alloromantic, and allosexual. People are pressured to fit that mold and feel that they must come out lest they be assumed to be an identity that they are not. Aro and ace people who have not come out can be placed into situations where they are pressured either to lie or come out, both of which can be very uncomfortable.

"[When I came out to] my two best friends, one of them was very positive: she had just figured out she's bi and that

she might be ace-spec in some way, so we could talk about LGBTQ+ stuff a lot. The other one 'doesn't really believe in labels' and asked all the questions of how I could be sure etc. which was very annoying and unsupportive but after some time she accepted it, though she did out me to some new acquaintances last year which is one of the reasons why she's an ex-best friend."—Birgit

OUR ADVICE

- You do not owe your identity to anyone, no matter how close you are with them.
- Remember that not coming out is not lying. Additionally, it is okay to lie to protect yourself, and it is important to prioritize your own safety and wellbeing over others' comfort.
- Outline your boundaries regardless of societal or friends' expectations, and strategize how to establish your boundaries in a friend group and elsewhere. You do not need to come out in order to set a boundary.
- Remember that no matter your identity, your boundaries deserve respect and your friends need to recognize that. If the friendship is healthy, your friends will want to understand and accommodate boundaries.
- If you choose to come out to your friends, plan out when and how you will do so. Consider their possible reactions and plan out how you might respond in those situations.
- If you want to come out to your friends in general, you do not have to do so all at once. You can start by telling one person or a few people about your identity. If the people you tell at first are affirming, they can support you as you continue your coming-out process.
- If your friends are not accepting, you are better off

without them, as painful as that may be. Pursue friendships in the aro and ace communities with people who will accept you or understand what you're going through. There are also aro and ace people in every community, with every identity, who enjoy all sorts of other activities and you could connect in additional ways completely irrelevant to your shared ace or aro identity.

Coworkers

Whether to come out at work is a question that many queer people confront multiple times in their lives, and aro and ace people are no exception. There are many factors that go into this decision—some apply across the LGBTQIA+ spectrum, such as the presence of non-discrimination laws in their state or country or their workplace's general track record related to diversity. However, some factors are ace- and aro-specific. Many aro and ace people don't ever come out to coworkers. Generally, they may not want to deal with any of the issues or fears listed above, and unlike all of the previous categories, coworkers are not people specifically chosen to be in one's life and are not often privy to deeply personal information. Further, they do not need that information to maintain a comfortable standard coworker relationship. However, romance may come up at social occasions, and workplace banter about sex or romantic lives can make ace or aro people uncomfortable, particularly if they feel they have to out themselves to convince coworkers to stop engaging in that kind of behavior. It may be particularly frustrating to romance-repulsed or romance-averse aromantic people, as it is usually considered inappropriate to speak about sex in the workplace but it is much harder to request that coworkers do not engage in conversation about romance. Additionally, some people may want to bring their "whole self" to work, including their ace or aro identity, but be afraid of direct or indirect consequences, rooted in bias, that could impact their livelihood, healthcare, or general workplace wellbeing.

> *"So far I haven't gotten any negative reactions to coming out. But I suppose I'm not out to everyone either, most of my family and friends know, but many of my coworkers do not. It's not that I'm hiding it, but it sometimes can be hard or awkward to bring up in conversations. For example, if you're gay, you can let someone know by saying you have a partner of the same gender when everyone is discussing significant others, but it's hard to butt in if you're aro/ace. If you say you don't have a partner or you're single, they'll try to reassure you that you'll find someone, if you say you'll never have a partner or explicitly say you're aro/ace, it can derail the conversation about partners and makes you look kind of rude."—Heather*

OUR ADVICE

- Know that you do not have to come out at work if you don't want to. It is good and valid to keep work life separate from personal life, and everyone—aro, ace, and allo—keeps some aspects of their personal lives separate from their work lives. Your coworkers do not need to know about your orientation if you are uncomfortable telling them.
- If you are worried that your boundaries will not be respected, contact your HR department. Reach out to someone you trust for help drafting your request or planning out your talking points if needed. You can use the resources listed in the Appendix to prepare what you will communicate or give these resources to HR.
- If you choose to come out at work but reside in a place that does not have employment protections

for LGBTQIA+ people, make sure that you are secure financially and in terms of your healthcare.

- Identify any potential allies who can help you advocate for the respect you deserve—these allies can include other queer coworkers or friendly coworkers.
- Some workplaces have "Employee Resource Groups" or other affinity groups for LGBTQIA+ staff members. If yours does, consider joining. It might be a safer place to come out, and you can consider seeking advice about coming out more publicly in the workplace.

Approaches to Coming Out as Ace or Aro

In this section, we will present various strategies for how to frame or structure situations where you come out to others. There is no single right way to come out; if you want to come out, you should use any strategies that feel most comfortable based on your personality and the context. These approaches will be more or less helpful in different scenarios, based on the factors mentioned above, including the kinds of fears you may have and the relationships involved. You can also draw from multiple approaches or use a different approach altogether.

Some strategies we suggest focus on the type of information you share—we call them "Content Approaches." Other strategies focus on the way you present the information, including the format and setting; these are "Attitude Approaches."

Content Approaches
LABEL-FIRST APPROACH

The strategy: You tell the other person your ace or aro label first, regardless of whether or not the other person knows what it means. After stating your label, you then do any necessary explaining of what it means and discuss the personal experiences that led you to identify that way.

Pros

- If the other person is familiar with the identity, it may cut down on the amount of explaining that you feel obligated to provide.
- It is clear what the conversation is about from the very start.
- The other person is not able to invalidate your experience before you get to the point of asserting your label.

Cons

- If the other person is not familiar with the identity, they may be very confused at the start.
- You do not have an opportunity to change course before fully coming out if the person responds badly, which you would if you took a different approach.
- It can be difficult to just dive into the conversation, without a preamble.
- If the other person is aware of the label and has a negative preconception of it, you will be operating against that while you explain yourself.

Example

Asahi: "Hey, we are with the college newspaper, and we are conducting a survey on sexually attractive qualities."
Saida: "Hey, I'm actually asexual, so this survey is not relevant to me."

EXPERIENCE-FIRST APPROACH

The strategy: You start by telling the other person about your experiences that led you to identify as ace or aro, and *then* tell the other person about the label that you use to describe your experiences.

Pros

- This approach sets up the other person to understand both the identity and why it is important to you.
- It allows for someone to change course if it seems that the other person is not receptive or is invalidating. You can stop the process by not telling them the label.

Cons

- This approach may be a little too personal depending on who you are coming out to.
- It allows for the other person to invalidate your experiences by saying something like "That's okay, you'll find the person you're attracted to," even if they are trying to be reassuring.
- They may not realize that this is a coming-out conversation.

Example

Taemin: "The hottest girl just walked by. Don't you agree she's so hot?"

Nelson: "For me, I must form a strong emotional connection with someone before I have the possibility of developing a sexual attraction towards them. So I'd say I experience sexual attraction differently than you just did. It's called demisexuality."

Taemin: "You know, I don't think I've heard anyone say that before, that's interesting. It's good to know that about you."

TESTING THE WATERS

The strategy: You first discuss the label with the other person before actually coming out to them. This discussion is an attempt to gauge how accepting the other person will be of your identity. This can include asking them if they have heard of asexuality or aromanticism or asking about common aromantic and asexual experiences.

Pros

- This can be a way of trying to discern how safe it is to come out to a person before actually risking the other person knowing.
- You can try this before being fully ready to come out and then use a different strategy later.
- The conversations put less pressure on you.

Cons

- Many people will be more open to the idea of asexuality and aromanticism once they realize that their loved one identifies that way. They might be more judgmental if they think that this is just a hypothetical conversation.
- It might be hard for you to respond to others' negative reactions in the moment without revealing your own identity.

Example

Fernando: "Hey, so I was in the depths of Tumblr and I came across this queer identity that I'd never heard of before. Have you ever heard of being aromantic?"

Anwar: "What is that? Someone who smells good? Or someone who doesn't date?"

Fernando: "It's actually a whole spectrum of people who experience romantic attraction or love differently than most other people. I'm sure there have been times where you haven't been romantically into someone, even though you might be sexually attracted to them or they might tick off all the boxes on your 'ideal partner' list. Well, for some people they might never be romantically interested in others."

Anwar: "Cool, good to know!"

Fernando: "And I'm aromantic."

Anwar: "I'm so glad you told me."

NO-LABEL APPROACH

The strategy: You describe your orientation(s) through experiences or through the definition, without ever actually putting a specific label or name to it.

Pros

- Some people do not feel a label is important or relevant to their identity experience. If that includes you, this strategy aligns with those feelings!
- This strategy allows for plausible deniability with someone who may have negative reactions towards anything perceived as queer.
- You only have to describe your own feelings, and you will not feel pressured to describe the variety of experiences in the aromantic or asexual communities.

Cons

- If the other person thinks of this as a personality trait rather than an orientation, they may be more likely to invalidate you and try to change your thoughts or behavior.

- You may feel that others don't take your identity as seriously without a label attached to it.
- You will not be able to refer to yourself as ace or aro in that person's presence without possibly having to come out again or explain what they are referring to.

Example

Iovania: "So I'm not interested in dating anyone ever, because I just don't see people that way."
Usagi: "Okay, I won't set you up with anyone then."

Attitude Approaches
CASUAL APPROACH
The strategy: You just drop your identity on the other person without necessarily making a big deal about it.

Pros

- This can mean a much less in-depth conversation, allowing you to simply mention your identity and allowing space for both people to process the interaction.
- This approach may be less nerve-wracking for you, as you do not have to prepare for an entire discussion or explanation.

Cons

- If the other person doesn't know much about asexuality or aromanticism, they might not feel comfortable asking for more details and thus not fully understand you.

- It connotes that you may not take the conversation that seriously, which can downplay how much you care about it.
- Alternatively, the other person may demand more details and be upset if you are not willing to provide them. This places you in a difficult spot where you feel forced or obligated to have a more serious conversation than the one you wanted, or planned, to have about your identity.

Example

Marcus: "Hey Jamie, what are your plans this weekend?"

Jamie: "Not much, I'm going to be meeting up with my asexual book club."

Marcus: "Hey, I didn't know you were asexual! Cool. What book are you reading?"

SIT-DOWN APPROACH

The strategy: You make the space for a conversation about your identity with the other person, where you are both focused on the topic and not on anything else.

Pros

- This setting tells the other person to take the conversation seriously and allows them the chance to ask questions.
- Both (or all) people in the conversation are not distracted, and the conversation can be planned to only happen when everyone is calm and in the right emotional space.

Cons

- You might not want to make the discussion such a big "identity reveal" conversation and might not feel comfortable discussing it in great detail.
- It may set both people up to be more emotional than is comfortable for them.
- You will have to deal with the reactions of the other person immediately, and if the other person reacts badly, the situation can quickly spiral into an unproductive or toxic interaction.

Example

Devon: "Dmitri, I have something important to talk to you about. Can we talk in private right now?"

Dmitri: "Sure, Devon. Is something wrong?"

Devon: "Nothing is wrong, but I've never told you this. I almost never feel romantic attraction. Whenever you talk about crushes, I can't really relate. I'm on the aromantic spectrum—specifically, grayromantic."

Dmitri: "Wow, Devon! This is clearly very important to you, so I'm so glad you're telling me now."

DISTANCE APPROACH

The strategy: You send a letter or email coming out, or make a phone call rather than speaking to the person face to face.

Pros

- This allows for some emotional and physical distance, particularly if safety is a concern.
- If making a call or using texts or instant messages, you can hang up before or when things become hostile to

quickly leave the situation. If you are sending an email or letter, you do not have to respond immediately, or at all, to someone else's negative reaction.

- This approach enables you to send links or write recommendations of other resources explaining your identity, which reduces the burden on you to explain and field questions.
- If it is in a written form, it is a more scripted approach and allows you to have more control over the scenario and put a lot of thought into what you express without being impacted by the real-time reactions of the person you're coming out to.

Cons

- It may not allow for the level of emotional connection that feels necessary.
- There will be a delay in reaction, which can be very nerve-wracking.
- The recipient may not ask all the same clarifying questions they would've otherwise asked in a face-to-face conversation, so it makes it harder for you to know what needs clarification.
- It may require a follow-up face-to-face conversation.
- The other person may research the orientation on their own and find misleading or incorrect information without your direction.
- It may be hard to interpret tone in a written form, so the other person might not understand your emotions or you might not understand the emotions in their response.

Example

Dear Dad,

I've been away at college for a few months now, and I've learned a lot about myself while I've been here. This may be a surprise to you, but I'm asexual and aromantic, which means I'm not attracted to anyone sexually or romantically. This is all very new to you, so I recommend learning more about these identities by buying this excellent book about the identities that I am linking you to, from an organization called The Ace and Aro Advocacy Project.

Also, I've recently signed up to be in the musical, and I'm very excited! And can you send me a care package of granola bars? The ones they sell here taste like cardboard.

Love,
Al

Appropriate Responses to Ace and Aro People Coming Out

"The best form of support I could receive is being granted respect and autonomy to know my own mind and make my own decisions rather than patronizing condescension regarding my choices. Part of the reason I don't acknowledge various minority identities I have is that I don't want people to treat me differently upon discovery. I feel that society today sees difference and, rather than trying to understand or nurture it, immediately tries to redirect it or stamp it out altogether. I wish more people would meet others where they are rather than trying to push them toward something else or erase them entirely."—CJ

Dos and Don'ts
When you come out as aro or ace, you may fear that the other person's response will be hurtful, invalidating, ignorant, or any of a range of negative responses. While we wish we could assure

you that that won't happen, it is very possible that someone will respond that way, whether intentionally or even as they are trying to be supportive or trying to understand. We have provided this list of "dos and don'ts" as a resource for you to share with others, as well as for you to keep in mind yourself if someone else comes out to you as ace or aro.

In this section, we are speaking directly to allo people.

Most of the general advice when a loved one or acquaintance comes out as aro or ace is the same as it would be for other LGBTQIA+ identities. Make it clear that your feelings for them haven't changed and you accept them for who they are, and thank them for trusting you with their identity. For many people, coming out can be a terrifying experience, and making an insensitive comment or joke, even if it's just because you don't know what to say or feel uncomfortable, can seriously impact both this person's relationship with you and their identity. If you have already made this kind of comment, apologize for it even if it's significantly after the fact, and explain the deeper understanding you've gained since then.

> *"I've come out to very few people. Those who I have are all queer, and they've all been nice, but I know they don't understand because they've [said] it. They make a lot of jokes, all lighthearted and I know they are not meant to be hurtful, but when it's all I hear, it just makes me want to be silent. I would love to talk about dating and trying to find a partner with them, but they can't separate that from wanting to have sex, so it's tough."—Anonymous*

There are also aspects to coming out as ace or aro that don't apply to many other identities. Therefore, even if you are supportive of other queer people or are even allo and queer yourself, you may learn something from these dos and don'ts.

Also, please see the "Common Issues and Fears" section earlier in this chapter to calibrate your response, and particularly pay attention to the list of invalidating comments included in the bingo cards in the Appendix.

Do	Don't
Make it clear that you are open to learning more about how this person identifies and how their identity manifests in their lives.	Expect them to be a walking encyclopedia; not everyone wants to give an introductory lecture to their identity to everyone they meet.
Feel free to do research into this identity.	Assume that everything you read will apply.
Allow the person to tell you about their own attractions and orientations in their own time, without any pressure.	Assume that their other forms of attraction either don't exist or are enhanced in some way. E.g. if someone comes out as ace, don't assume that they don't have romantic feelings. If someone comes out as aro, don't assume that they have a greater sex drive.
Listen to all they choose to explain to you openly and without prejudice.	Expect them to be able to explain attraction; they are telling you that they do not feel attraction and are likely to not understand what "romantic attraction" feels like as an aromantic person or "sexual attraction" as asexual person.
Match their tone when coming out; if they treat the conversation as casual, do the same, and if they treat it seriously, you should as well.	Make a joke or diminish or invalidate their identities in any way, no matter how casually they may come out.
Ensure they know you accept them and you are happy they shared their identity with you.	Assume that they are waiting for your validation or approval by telling them you are okay with their identity.
Give them the chance to explain what they expect from you and what, if any, behaviors they want you to change.	Presume to know their limitations or boundaries around specific behaviors based on their attractions.

ORIENTATIONS ARE FLUID

As discussed in Chapter 1, sexual and romantic orientations can be fluid. This absolutely should not be used as a reason for invalidating anyone's orientation. For example, imagine someone telling an individual that being straight is "just a phase" or "might change." These phrases are often used to invalidate gay, bi, and other queer people, and many people now recognize that this is wrong, rude, and invasive. However, these phrases are still used to invalidate aro and ace people, even by those who would never use them to invalidate anyone of any other orientation. Ace and aro people are commonly told that they should keep their minds open, since they might meet someone who changes their identity. This is equally unacceptable.

Despite this caveat, it is still true that people's orientations can change, but it's important not to suggest that possibility to someone unless they are already bringing it up themselves and not to use the concept of fluidity as an excuse to invalidate their orientations.

This becomes a trap for ace and aro people especially. If Saoirse used to identify as a lesbian both sexually and romantically, but now identifies as homosexual and aromantic, others might assume that she "just wants to sleep around" or that she faced some trauma in her previous relationships that lead her to refuse to enter into a new relationship. On the other hand, if Sanjay identifies as aroace at the age of 16, people might tell him that he just hasn't had enough life experience and he'll meet the right person someday, implying that his orientations are fluid when instead they are very fixed. No matter their life experiences, Saoirse and Sanjay's orientations are and should be seen as valid, and should not be questioned by anyone but Saoirse and Sanjay themselves.

Specific Advice for Different Audiences

Generally, when someone who is asexual or aromantic comes out, fundamental dos and don'ts apply across the board, regardless of audience. However, there are additional things to keep in mind depending on one's role in the life of a person who has decided to come out. For general dos and don'ts, see the previous section. What follows is specific advice for those with various relationships with those on the asexual or aromantic spectrums.

PARTNERS

- Seek to fully understand your asexual or aromantic partner's comfort level for participating in sexual and romantic activities, as well as the circumstances, if any, under which they may experience sexual or romantic attraction.
- Within both the aro and ace communities, there exists a large amount of diversity in preferences. A partner, if demi- or graysexual, or demi- or grayromantic, may experience sexual and/or romantic attraction under some limited circumstances. The degree to which a partner on the asexual or aromantic spectrum is willing to engage in sexual or romantic activities depends on whether they are sex- or romance-favorable, neutral, averse, or repulsed.
- Remember, some who are asexual enjoy sex, and some who are aromantic enjoy romance. Action does not equal attraction, and not all ace and aro people define their identity around attraction.
- Do not assume that your partner will necessarily never agree to sex or romance, and communicate with your partner regarding their wishes.
- Do not assume that your partner is not capable of love.

- Similar principles apply in determining whether your partner may have interest in raising a child with you. Some agree to have sex simply for the purpose of conceiving a child. Some are interested in raising a child without using sex as a method of conception—e.g. through adoption, surrogacy, IVF, etc.
- Determine basic ground rules for who will initiate various sexual and romantic activities, as well as ways to show the presence and absence of consent.
- Discuss all partners' needs in the relationship and identify any areas of conflicting needs. Only at this point should you then make decisions about whether the relationship should continue in its current form and perhaps consider whether less mainstream options such as a queerplatonic or polyamorous relationship might be right for your particular situation.

FAMILY

- Begin to come to terms with any decision your relative might make regarding family planning, with respect to their orientation. Though many on the asexual and aromantic spectrums do marry and have children, many choose not to follow traditional paths of union and child-rearing.
- Do not invalidate your relative's orientation because you might never become an aunt, grandparent, father-in-law, etc. Keep the focus of the discussion on the person coming out. The decision to marry or have children does not rest with anyone outside of those deciding whether to marry or raise a child.
- Do not assume that your relative will be alone forever, and do not assume that "being alone forever" is necessarily something that will cause your relative

distress. Ace and aro people form all kinds of fulfilling relationships, which may or may not include traditional partnerships; for those who are not interested in a long-term romantic relationship such as a marriage, respect their decision and trust that they know their own needs and desires.

- Given that evidence shows that orientation is largely, if not entirely, a question of nature rather than nurture, do not begin to assume that something could have been done during the rearing process to prevent the person coming out from having their particular sexual and romantic preferences or begin to harbor guilt regarding any responsibility during the upbringing of the person coming out with respect to their orientation. In addition, any guilt may signal to your relative that you think there is something inherently wrong with their orientation, invalidating and harming them.

- Make an effort to prevent a decline in quality of the relationship due to denial of the validity of asexuality and aromanticism.

- If you find that you may be, or are, the only person within your entire family who supports, or would support, your relative coming out, discuss how you plan to proceed as an ally with the person coming out, including who will find out about your relative's orientation, when they will find out, and responses to the possible reactions from other relatives.

DOCTORS AND THERAPISTS

- Stay up to date on scholarly research on topics relevant to asexuality and aromanticism, as relevant to your specialty, as well as available resources to assist those identifying under these umbrellas.

- When a client or patient comes out to you, inquire about their awareness of resources designed for those on the asexual and aromantic spectrums, and ask if they would like you to recommend any resources. Ask occasionally if there is any way you may assist in any of the challenges particular to those on the asexual and/or aromantic spectrum, while doing your best to refrain from appearing overbearing or infantilizing.
- Similarly, if you sense that a client or patient may be as asexual or aromantic but lacks awareness of these orientations, bring up the possibility, as well as helpful resources.[7] Also inquire as to whether the patient or client would like to address any struggles in navigating the world with their orientation as part of their work with you.
- Evaluate protocol within your practice, such as the recommended timing of pap smears or screenings for sexually transmitted infection (STIs), to determine whether your recommendations accommodate asexual and aromantic clients and patients, and adjust accordingly.
- Make sure forms, where relevant, allow those you serve to accurately describe their orientations, using a fill-in-the-blank format, and strive to provide inclusive informational materials.
- Do not pressure your clients or patients to, or assume that your clients or patients plan to, have children.
- Do not assume that your patient or client is using a label(s) under the asexual or aromantic umbrella as a way to transition towards identifying with a different orientation.
- Do not pathologize your client or patient's orientation,

---

7   See "Bringing Up the Possibility" in Chapter 5.

and do not invalidate their orientation based on any pre-existing conditions you may be aware of. However, if desired, you may gently discuss the idea that some people do perceive the unique intersections of experiences with trauma or a specific disability identity with their experience of asexuality or aromanticism to be salient parts of their identity, taking extra caution to avoid any pathologization.

FRIENDS

- Ask your friend how you can best support them.
- Be cognizant of any assumptions you may make about your friend's plans to marry, have children, engage in casual sex, view pornographic materials, or have discussions about any of these topics, and learn your friend's specific preferences where relevant.
- Make an effort to include and accommodate your friend when it comes to planning activities where one is expected to bring a date or partner.
- Discuss a plan with the person coming out regarding others with whom you may share your social circle.
- Do not assume that your friend will necessarily never enjoy speaking about, or consuming media on topics related to, sexuality and romance and that they will necessarily shy away from platonic touch.
- Begin to reflect on your notions of what it means to be a significant other, realize that friendships can contain just as much emotional intimacy as romantic and sexual partnerships, and rethink any notions of ranking platonic and non-platonic relationships with respect to quality, depth, and level of commitment.

COWORKERS

- Strive for inclusivity when planning outings and activities, such as for Valentine's Day, and make it easy to opt out.
- Do not assume that any coworker's job performance is affected by their orientation.
- Additionally, do not assume anything about your coworker's life trajectory.
- If you see any harassment, invalidation, or discrimination taking place, speak up, even if anonymously. However, be careful not to out your colleague if they are not out publicly at work. Additionally, be careful and intentional when you report these things if your area does not have inclusive employment discrimination protection laws.
- Try to ensure that any informational materials produced by your workplace are inclusive.

Coming out can be an incredibly affirming experience to an aro or ace person, bolstering their feelings of self-worth and helping them feel more fully seen and understood by the people in their life. A person coming out usually must first be confident enough in their identity to share it with others and have accepted their orientation as a significant part of their overall identity. Choosing not to come out at all or selectively coming out, while not the focus of this section, can also be affirming, as it can afford the individual agency, privacy, and safety. Some people may not come out simply because their identity is not relevant or important to them or their relationship with those around them, and that is a legitimate choice as well. Choosing not to come out is also not necessarily a permanent decision, as some people may choose to come out later—whether because their circumstances have changed, their acceptance of their identity has changed, or for some other reason. Coming out also happens repeatedly in many ace and aro individuals' lives, as they have many people they interact with, new people they'll meet, and new understandings of their own orientations to share.

Coming out is expected of non-straight people in our heteronormative society, and the performative aspect of it can be freeing for some and pointless for others. It is certainly not the end of the process of embracing an ace or aro identity. That comes in the next part of the process, when the person has integrated their orientation into their overall identity, and it is no longer a focus, while still remaining relevant to who they are as a person.

CHAPTER 10

Part Seven—Identity Integration

Identity integration occurs separately from one accepting their ace or aro identity and instead is about the specific conceptualization of this identity within the context of the rest of one's sense of self. Often identity integration is about a deeper level of acceptance of the identity or even a feeling of pride in the identity. The aro or ace individual begins to process their aro or ace identity as one of their many personal traits. They are no longer very interested in changing themselves or conforming to societal or familial expectations. An ace or aro person may finally feel they are able to recognize the amatonormativity and compulsory sexuality within their societal context and feel liberated at how identifying with an ace or aro label is a way to lessen the pressure of these norms. At this point, people may come out differently. They may be more casual about it, not thinking too much about potential consequences, as it is just part of their everyday life. Something that may have been much more anxiety inducing may now be expressed without forethought.

Community Involvement

The identity integration part of the process is also the time when many people begin to invest time more fully into aro or ace communities, discussed in Chapters 2 and 7, as they now feel like they could be a full member. The experiences of this final part can sometimes happen before other parts and other times not happen at all. Many people may struggle to find community, and while this part of the process is a goal for many, it may be better to focus on smaller and more attainable goals such as simply being comfortable using the aro or ace label for yourself. This comfort can mean many different things to different people.

There is no single "correct" path for an ace or aro person coming to terms with their identity.

> "I accept my ace/aro identity, but I'm not all that passionate about it. Maybe that's because I've never been forced to defend my position regarding my sexuality, but in general it plays a relatively small role in my life."—CJ

Sometimes being ace or aro is not something relevant to many aspects of your life, and you don't see it as a significant enough part of your sense of self to even bother wanting to come out—and that's completely fine! Straight people who are both allosexual and alloromantic don't usually have to think about their identity in the course of their days or let it impact how they live. You don't need to be active in aro, ace, or other LGBTQIA+ spaces to identify as such. If the orientation isn't important in your life, or is less important than other aspects of who you are, you can push it out of your mind altogether if you want. Your orientation doesn't need to be considered an identity as much as a small, descriptive detail about your experiences. Alternatively, you may see your ace or aro identity as significant, yet entirely personal and about your own understanding of yourself rather than relevant to interpersonal interactions. You don't need to pressure yourself to be more "visibly" aro or ace; you don't need to perform your orientation in order for you to feel comfortable with it.

Some aro or ace people are very loud about their orientation(s), express a great deal of pride, and may consider their orientation(s) an extremely important part of who they are. (Some of them are writing this book.) That's also an awesome way to be! If you want to, and feel safe to, emphasize your identity to others, write it on your social media profile, or wear lots of pride gear, there's no reason not to. It can feel incredibly powerful and reaffirming to do that and can help fight off feelings of shame or vulnerability around an orientation. It can also help you find a community of other aro or ace people, as well as others who are affirming, as it will be easier for them to find you when you are constantly talking about how great being aro or ace is.

This chapter discusses the ways in which you may succeed or struggle with integrating your ace or aro identity, particularly within your greater social context or peer group and depending on how confident you feel about your identity. No one experiences an aro or ace identity in a vacuum, and how others perceive and treat your various identities always influences identity integration, regardless of whether those others are in the aro or ace community or outside of the community. Additionally, aro and ace people represent the full spectrum of human diversity—we are among all races, ethnicities, cultures, genders, disabilities, religions, nationalities, ages, socioeconomic classes, language-based communities, geographical communities, and more—and so many of the challenges and opportunities here will differ based on your other identities and the privileges you may or may not have. Being able to integrate your identity is influenced by your other traits and identities, as well as if your communities accept and encourage you to integrate your aro or ace identity.

Context Can Affect Integration
Being Confident Without Community Support

One issue that many ace and aro people face when trying to integrate their identity is that while they themselves may feel confident in their identities, they may not have a community that supports them or allows them to express their identities safely.

One's cultural community or peer group may be the one that is unsupportive. In Western countries, this may be more common for people of color and children of immigrants. Asexuality and aromanticism, like many other LGBTQIA+ identities, are often considered "Western" or "white." Aros and aces of color may find that their families believe them to be following a trend or trying to "act white," and they may struggle to explain to their families that these orientations can occur regardless of color or national origin. Also, ace and aro people from certain religious backgrounds may be accused of going against their beliefs or practices if their religious community views their aro or ace identity as incompatible with their belief system. Any presumed obstacle to the ideal heterosexual, romantic, monogamous, nuclear family may be seen as antithetical to certain religious ideals.

Aro and ace people may also experience a lack of support from communities that they expect to be affirming, such as LGBTQIA+ communities. Some LGBTQIA+ community spaces are unsupportive due to bias against or a lack of knowledge of ace and aro identities. Eventually, some may come across a supportive community after more searching, and some may even establish a community space themselves. However, having a community that supports one's ace or aro identity, while preferable, is not always necessary for self-assurance. Others go on to find fulfillment in things other than community.

Even when an aro or ace person is fully integrated and confident in their own identity, there could still be a sense of sadness and distress because their community and society have not caught up with their own sense of openness and acceptance towards ace, aro, and other queer identities. This does not necessarily come from people with different identities. Ace and aro communities may be hostile towards certain expressions and kinds of aro and ace identities or towards other identities that ace and aro people have, such as certain ethnicities and gender identities.

Some ace and aro people may face violence for having integrated with or accepted their identity. This can require an aro or ace person to go back in the closet or to start searching for more private ways of expressing their identity, such as only engaging with online communities, possessing subtle pride gear, or traveling long distances to engage in pride events far from their family and daily community.

People who have strongly integrated their aro or ace identity but have found little support may be more likely to engage in activism and advocacy. Having little support and acceptance from one's peer group can drive people to try to create more positive and accepting communities for other ace and aro people. Not every person in this scenario will become an activist, although the community of aro and ace activists contains many people who have this experience.

Not everyone will create their own community or find a current one that is acceptable. Some people may choose simply to not prioritize having support for their ace or aro identity. For some, this change in priorities and lack of community will be extremely difficult. For others, this may be the simplest or only path forward. If you are not interested in creating or finding community, you do not need to do so.

"I've hung around the outside of ace communities on Tumblr. I'm not really a community person tbh. They all seem to think of it as more of a big deal than I do. I mean, it *is* a core

aspect of my personality, but that doesn't mean I have to spend a whole load of time talking about it. I've got books to write and dancing to do instead."—Marnie

Not Being Confident and Not Having Community Support

A lack of community support makes it hard to attain personal identity integration. Near constant microaggressions, invalidation, and outright rejection may chip away at one's self-esteem, self-worth, and sense of feeling like their ace or aro experience is valid. Many people experience extreme peer pressure to conform to heteronormative, sex-normative, and amatonormative ideals. Due to this, they may not believe or trust their own internal experiences of lacking attraction or certain desires.

It is impossible for an ace or aro individual who considers their identity to be important to them to be completely integrated into a community that won't accept their identity. It is difficult for an individual to internally reach comfort with and acceptance of themself as a whole, cohesive being without some amount of community support. Ace and aro communities may be able to provide the support that the individual needs, although it may be difficult for that community to provide sufficient support to override the invalidation received from many other people in that individual's life. If one cannot find supportive community spaces, they may be able to find certain individuals who are willing and able to provide affirmation, encouragement, and support. If not having a community is distressing to you, see Chapter 2 for more advice on locating communities locally or online.

Not Being Confident but Having Community Support

Even with community support, it can be hard to have confidence in one's own ace or aro identity for multiple reasons. While community support can help normalize and validate aro and ace identities, there can still be a great deal of invalidation and other negativity outside these communities that make it hard to fully embrace one's identity. Even in situations where one's identity is accepted completely, there can still be lingering doubts derived from internalized acephobia and arophobia or from a wider sense of otherness from general society or even other members of the community. If other community members are mostly or entirely of different demographics—for example, if they are all much older or are all of a different gender or race than the person in question—this sense of still not fitting in can be even greater. Someone might see other people in their community as being more confident in their identity than they themself are, and wonder if their identity is as valid. They may thus feel they should be able to know their own identity for certain, without any doubts. A similar worry can result if someone has aspects of their identity, behavior, or presentation that, while accepted in the community, are uncommon or do not match the "standard" idea of an ace or aro identity—for example, an aro person who wants to date, while most aro people around them do not. The ace or aro person may also have a more limited idea of aro or ace identities and end up excluding themself, despite their communities' acceptance.

If someone doesn't feel confident in their identity, they may reject community support by, for example, going to fewer meetups or changing internet browsing habits to avoid ace and aro community spaces. When one is not confident in their identity, interacting with a community based around that identity can feel like living a lie, even, or especially, when they know that community would accept them, and they may worry about being found to be a "fake" aro or ace who doesn't belong. Someone might wait until they have integrated their identity internally before interacting much or coming out, even in an accepting community, due to an unwarranted or irrational fear of judgment about the validity of their identity. If someone goes as far as to cut themself off entirely from an accepting community, their experience might begin to look more like the previous section, "Not Being Confident and Not Having Community Support." If you have access to a supportive community but do not feel confident in your identity, use the resources in prior chapters that may help you develop greater self-esteem and self-acceptance.

> *"I absolutely wish I wasn't ace most days. I feel that I'm missing a part of myself, that I'm not whole or that I'm broken. As cliche as it is, it's something that constantly bothers me and keeps me from embracing myself. When I try to resolve those feelings, I often create a pro/con list and encourage myself to feel proud of the benefits of being asexual. Other times, I'll hop onto social media and scroll through some LGBTQ+ accounts for uplifting pictures and accepting people. [...] I feel proud of my identity when I'm with other LGBTQ+ people, and it's pretty amazing when we're all together. I like to tell my point of view and listen to others'. Pride events and communities are essential for me to really express myself and the pride for who I am."—Lauren*

Being Confident with Community Support

Being confident with community support is the ideal scenario, although unfortunately it is not possible for everyone. People in this category understand and accept their aro or ace identity, even if they occasionally feel self-doubt or are confused. They accept their orientation for what it is and are no longer trying to conform to compulsory sexuality or amatonormative standards. They have at least some people around them who also accept and understand their identity and expression, whether or not they are aware of the individual's specific identity labels; for example, if the ace or aro person does not feel the need to be out about their identity labels in particular but is still supported in their identity expression. These people may be family, friends, partners, coworkers, or other LGBTQIA+ people.

People in this category may be active in ace or aro communities, potentially through blogging, creating art, or doing community outreach and advocacy. They may have a sense of pride in their identity and may show that by displaying pride paraphernalia such as flags, pins, and other things discussed in Chapter 2. However, this sense of pride is not reactionary as it might be in Part Five, when they might denigrate other orientations as part of that pride. Rather, it is feeling joyful about one's own identity and what it brings them. They can be part of communities that support others who are less confident in their orientation.

> *"I participate in the ace community online through a Tumblr blog. There I provide resources and information about asexuality (and other identities) and talk about my own experiences. I also help people who have questions or need help figuring themselves out. The blog has been an extremely positive experience in my life. It has helped me accept myself and come to terms with being asexual, and it has also given me pride in my identity. Helping people like me has inadvertently helped myself, and I am grateful."—Alyssa*

Conversely, they may be comfortable with their identity to the point that they no longer think about it and it is not a focus of their activities or conversations. They may not feel the need to connect with other aro or ace individuals or with those communities. The concept of "pride" may be completely irrelevant for them—in the same way that some people have pride in their hometown while others would view that as a foreign concept.

Neither form of identity integration is superior, as they are both forms of accepting and internalizing an identity. At this point, one's asexuality, aromanticism, or both take their place among other identities rather than being separated from or irreconcilable with one's overall sense of self due to questioning or insecurity.

> *"I feel secure about my identity (though a relationship and actually enjoying sex with my partner have pushed my boundaries of my initial self-identification) but I don't tend to be too vocal about this part of myself. This has nothing to do with shame though, I just believe it to belong to the private sphere and not something I like to broadcast. However, my closest friends are definitely aware of my identity."—Jess*

CHAPTER 11

Conclusion

Non-Linearity of Identity Integration

Sometimes people go through the parts of the process in exactly the order we've outlined above, and after they get through Part Seven, their ace or aro identity is forever integrated into the rest of their sense of self. This section isn't about them.

Many, even most, people do not experience the parts of embracing an aro or ace identity in quite such a simple way. People continuously discover and rediscover their identities. Even if they are confident in their own desires, attractions, feelings, or lack thereof, the community they are in may shift its understanding of that identity. If they change communities, they may have to re-establish the way they define their ace or aro identity and reintegrate it into their overall sense of self. They may also discover new feelings, desires, or attractions that make them shift or question their understanding of their identities.

Sometimes this is due to linguistic shifts in the community. For example, "aromantic" used to commonly mean no romantic attraction at all, with aro and arospec as more general phrases that covered the entire spectrum of identities. That is how we use those words in this book. However, in many circles, "aromantic" now means the entirety of the aro community, including those who experience romantic attraction occasionally. This has led some no-attraction aromantic people to create new terminology for themselves, including terms like "end-spec aro." Just redefining one's personal aromantic identity in this context requires a certain level of new identity integration and may cause a revisit to Part Two, Discovery of Terminology.

Changes in the lives of people around an aro or ace person may also impact their understanding of their identity. For example, someone who is asexual may not think that their identity impacts their relationships with friends much when they're younger, as most of their friends then are not sexually active or comfortable talking about sex. However, they may feel differently about their identity and how it changes their relationships with others when they get older and begin inter-acting with people who frequently talk about and want to hear about sexual activity. That alone could potentially cause them to swing back up to Parts Three, Identity Confusion, or Five, Identity Acceptance and Salience Negotiation. Just meeting new people will often cause ace and aro people to re-enter Part Six, Coming Out.

The reexamination of your identity, for whatever reasons, even though it may cause some people to feel like they are backsliding or losing any sense of progress, is valid and is in fact an important part of making further progress. Reexamining and integrating your identity is often a lifelong process and does not need to be frightening or something that prevents you from moving forward. Rather, reintegrating identity, or moving through any of the parts in this book multiple times, can lead to a deeper, more meaningful sense of self.

Questioning

You may have started this book unsure of your identity or where you fit in aro or ace communities—we hope that we've given you some tools to think about your orientations or to learn more. But if you still aren't sure, that's okay! It's okay to keep questioning, potentially forever. It's also okay to pick a label that seems best, even if it's not perfect, or even to pick a label that represents not feeling sure, such as quoiromantic or nebulasexual.

All of these experiences are extremely subjective—it's nearly impossible to perfectly map one person's understanding of attraction, sexuality, romance, needs, or desires onto somebody else's. In many cases, the best you can do is approximate your experiences with a label, which may only encompass certain aspects of what you think is most important. This helps explain the proliferation of different microlabels to describe very specific experiences. If you want to use multiple labels, you can, even if they seem contradictory.

On the other hand, if you want to just identify with the overarching labels of "ace" or "aro" (or both), you can do that without needing to specify further—more than that, you can identify as "queer" alone or choose not to use any labels for your romantic or sexual orientations if that makes most sense to you. If you can't or don't want to specify your orientations but you still feel connected with aro or ace communities, you can still participate in any way that feels right to you—whether that means relating to the experiences described in this book, consuming ace or aro media, feeling like some aspect of the labels apply to you, or joining an aro or ace group. Whatever your reasons, welcome to the club, and we're so glad you found us!

> "For those questioning,
>
> It's okay to take your time. It's okay to doubt. Just remember. You are ultimately the one who knows yourself best. Don't let anyone doubt you, not for too long, that is."—Haven

Positivity

A lot of this book may have been intense or difficult to read—some of the experiences of coming to understand or embrace an aro or ace identity can be painful or exhausting. But we do not want you to come away thinking that ace and aro identities are only sources of challenge and pain. As this book comes to a close, we want to leave you with some joy. Overall, everyone involved with writing this book does feel a sense of joy in their identity and is happy to have found the community—as are so many other ace and aro people across the world, including most of the people we quoted in this book. We hope that you feel a similar sense of joy in your identity or at least look forward to a time when you can feel that joy.

"Since I found out I was ace, I haven't felt broken like I did before. I haven't felt alone like I did before."—Tom

"I do feel very proud of my aro identity. I feel like it has helped me look at life in a different, more down-to-earth and realistic way, and it opened my mind to other experiences as well."—Circus

"I enjoy exploring sexuality and how people express and define their experiences. I love the nuance and detail we are starting to understand when it comes to our expressions and experiences of attraction, desire, and arousal. I have found the LGBTQIA and ace/aro communities are particularly adept at delineating between various experiences and concepts which in turn has helped me to develop better communication and understanding of myself and others. Each Asexual Awareness Week (in October in the UK) I try to share some of the wisdom I've found within these communities as I firmly believe that heterosexuals would benefit from understanding the differences between sexual attraction, desire, aesthetic attraction

*and arousal better in the same way that I know my monoga-
mous relationship has greatly benefitted from learning and
understanding about polyamorous relationships."—Megan*

*"I think the best (actual) part of being acespec and arospec and
having those words as an identity is that it gives me a framework to understand and discuss my experiences with people.
It also allows me to better understand myself and my needs.
For example, I can identify and avoid a conversation that
makes me uncomfortable and then bring up my discomfort
with someone later to set a clearer boundary."—Anonymous*

*"Since I began to identify as aro, I have felt very positive
about it. I have been learning as much as I can about other
people's experiences, rethinking some of my experiences and
have joined an LGBTIQA+ group. I've noticed that I am less
touch-averse lately, especially with men. I also worry less
about having my feelings invalidated or fending off romantic approaches, because being able to say 'I'm aro' gives me
a way to describe what I feel. I am very happy to have this
identity."—Victoria*

*"I don't feel proud or better for being asexual or aroman-
tic. I feel lucky for being asexual and aromantic because
these orientations align well with the rest of my personal
features."—Isaac*

*"It's always nice to find fellow aro allosexuals. I thought I
was on my own for so long, and it was like a whole new world
opening up when I found other people online."—AD Stewart*

*"I feel really good knowing what I am! I love it. I feel that I
know myself more now than ever before. I wouldn't say that
I am 'proud' of it. That is like thinking you are better than*

everyone else—that's what I think, but I feel good knowing it and knowing me."—Luna

"I definitely like the feeling of my experiences finally 'clicking,' of the things I've thought and been through making sense, of finding a community that experiences things similarly. Probably my happiest moment of Ace Pride was when I went to my first pride parade, last summer. I was there with my friend and we scouted out the one booth that was selling an ace flag. After taking it out of the package, I tied it around my shoulders and ran around the green shouting 'I'm an Asexual Super Hero!' and the people sitting near us cheered."—Jamie M

"The pride for me comes from having done the hard, painstaking work of figuring out who I am. As an aromantic person I feel more comfortable in my own skin than I used to. I no longer feel damaged or emotionally defective or mentally ill for my desire to stay single and not enter romantic relationships."—Carl

"Being able to identify as aro/ace is hard sometimes, but it is something I have always internally loved about myself. I like who I am. I like being part of such a wonderful orientation with such a wonderful community built around it. I have felt a lot more confident about myself and what I want after I started identifying because it allows me to know and express who I am and what I want on my terms. I am very proud of being aro/ ace even though it is not easy."—Rivers

"When I found the terms aro [and] ace and the community, a weight was lifted and I cried. I'd never felt so at home with a way of thinking/life. Very proud!"—DoctorBBQ

"I love having an identity that answers so many questions I was asking about myself. The anxiety and confusion is no

longer an issue, and it becomes easier to plan my life goals knowing that I am different (i.e. when it comes to parenthood). That's the purpose of an identity for me, to make your feelings [and] value[s] official, either to just yourself or publicly. I think a lot of people get fed up with how many identities there are out there and how confusing it can all get, but if I didn't have an identity I would be suffering. I would be confused and ashamed of myself. That's why I love having something I can turn to and saying 'Yep, this is why I am the way I am, and I'm okay with that.'"—Anonymous

Glossary

TAAAP has defined all the words and terms below in as comprehensive a way as possible. However, because language, particularly in aro and ace communities, is always evolving, different people will have different definitions and understandings of these terms. We do not deny the validity of other definitions, but the most general understanding of these words, to our knowledge, is given in the definitions that follow.

Ace-spec: generally refers to someone who identifies within the ace community, and is explicitly inclusive of the entire spectrum of identities under the asexual umbrella. (Not to be confused with the term "aspec.")

Acegender: any gender identity influenced by an asexual or asexual spectrum identity. It can be used as an umbrella or as a label in itself.

Acephobia: a hatred of, dislike of, fear of, or prejudice against asexual people and identities, as well as concepts commonly associated with asexuality.

Aego and autochoris (sexual/romantic): two prefixes both used to describe people who may have fantasies and enjoy the idea of sexual or romantic activities but do not wish to be a participant themselves. They feel a disconnect between themselves and the concept of attraction or relationships, and they may only enjoy the hypothetical concept when it's a situation they couldn't possibly be in (e.g. they may enjoy porn or romance novels but possess no desire to participate in the activities depicted).

Aesthetic attraction: the feeling that something pleases the senses. It is usually visual but can also be auditory or olfactory, or relate to any of the senses.

AFAB: assigned female at birth; generally born with a vagina.

Agender: a specific nonbinary or genderqueer identity for people who do not identify with any gender at all or with the concept of gender.

Alloace or alloro ace: shorthand for people who are both alloromantic and on the asexual spectrum; often referred to as "romantic asexual."

Allonormativity: the assumption, belief, and expectation that people experience romantic and sexual attraction and that feeling these attractions are the "default" or "norm." It is predicated on the idea that asexual and aromantic identities do not exist.

Alloro allo (allo) (allo2) (allorose): shorthand for people who are not on the asexual or aromantic spectrums, who are allosexual and alloromantic.

Alloromantic (alloro): people who are not on the aromantic spectrum.

Allosexual (allo): people who are not on the asexual spectrum.

Alterous attraction: a desire for some form of emotional closeness with a specific person that cannot be described either as romantic or platonic.

AMAB: assigned male at birth; generally born with a penis.

Amatonormativity: the disproportionate focus on and prioritization of romantic relationships above all else and the widespread assumption that finding romantic love is a universally shared goal. Amatonormativity describes the systemic way in which these sociocultural ideas and norms are upheld—this includes the formal institution of marriage and the many legal benefits it confers.

Aphobia: a hatred of, dislike of, fear of, or prejudice against aromantic and asexual people and identities, as well as concepts commonly associated with aromanticism and asexuality.

Aplatonic (apl): people who experience little to no platonic attraction or desire, or feel disconnected from the concept of platonic relationships.

Arospec: generally refers to someone who identifies within the aro community, and is explicitly inclusive of the entire spectrum of identities under the aromantic umbrella.

Aroace (or AroAce or aro ace): shorthand for people who are on both the aromantic and asexual spectrums.

Aroallo or alloaro: shorthand for people who are both on the aromantic spectrum and allosexual.

Arogender: any gender identity influenced by an aromantic or aromantic spectrum identity. It can be used as an umbrella or as a label in itself.

Aromantic (aro): people who experience little to no romantic attraction or desire, or feel disconnected from the concept or category of romance.

Arophobia: a hatred of, dislike of, fear of, or prejudice against aromantic people and identities, as well as concepts commonly associated with aromanticism.

Arousal or sexual arousal: physical excitement usually associated with sexuality and an expression of libido. Also known as "horniness" or being "turned on."

Asexual (ace): people who experience little to no sexual attraction or desire, or feel disconnected from the concept or category of sexuality.

Aspec or a-spec: an umbrella term for anyone who identifies as part of the asexual or aromantic spectrums. (Not to be confused with the term "ace-spec.")

Bi: describes people who are attracted to or oriented towards more than one gender, multiple genders, or all genders. The most common differentiation between bi and pan orientations is that bi people are attracted to multiple genders, though that attraction may be different depending on the gender, while pan people are attracted no matter the gender. However, this distinction is not universal.

While bisexual is an orientation label that is commonly used to encompass a variety of attractions, the bi- prefix may be used to refer to any one specific kind of attraction, such as biromantic, bi-alterous, bi-sexual, specifically in reference to sexual attraction, or bi-platonic.

Cisgender (cis): describes people who identify as the gender they were assigned at birth.

Cisnormativity: the assumption that everyone is cisgender or identifies as the gender they were assigned at birth. It involves base assumptions of gender roles, stereotypes, expectations, and norms, and people are judged by the perception of their conformity (or lack thereof)—for example, based on gender presentation.

Come out: when a person discloses that they are one or more identities in the LGBTQIA+ umbrella. For many people, coming out is an ongoing, lifelong process. People may choose to come out to certain people or in certain contexts only; others may choose to come out to everyone in their lives, sometimes at the same time.

Compulsory sexuality: the societal assumption reinforced by social norms and institutions that everyone feels sexual attraction and desire to some extent. This also includes the pressure to act on those feelings and the incorporation of sex into societal expectations about major phases of life.

Closeted or in the closet: when someone privately identifies as an LGBTQIA+ identity but does not tell others about their identity or identities. Being closeted is the opposite of being out. Someone can be closeted in all situations or only in certain situations (e.g. out to their friends but closeted at work).

Consent: agreement to do or be involved in something; is often referred to in the context of sexual or romantic interactions. Must be reaffirmed for each new action taken, as consent for one action does not necessarily mean consent for any other action. Verbal consent is the clearest form of consent, but consent can come in other forms.

Crush: experiencing romantic attraction towards someone specific. May be used as a noun (one's crush) or a verb (crushing on). May also involve forms of attraction besides romantic.

Cupio (sexual/romantic): people who do not experience a specific attraction but still desire to form that kind of relationship.

Demi (sexual/romantic): people who do not experience attraction unless a strong emotional bond has been formed first. The emotional connection is a necessary but not sufficient factor.

Demigender: an identity that describes people who do not feel a full or complete connection to a gender but feel some amount or a partial connection to that gender. Many people identify the gender in question by adding the gender label after demi, such as demigirl, demiboy, or demigenderfluid.

End-spec (ace/aro): someone who identifies as having no (sexual or romantic) attraction or desire at all. It refers to being at the extreme "end" of the sexual or romantic spectrum, and it implicitly respects all identities within the spectrum, including people who feel some levels of attraction.

Feminine: a set of attitudes, behaviors, or roles commonly associated with women and girls. Note that this is different depending on culture, as there are different associations with women in different cultural contexts, and that being a woman is not the same as being feminine. Persons of any gender can take on any and all characteristics of being feminine.

Fluid (orientation): people who connect with the idea that their orientation is not fixed but rather has changed, does change, or might change. It also refers to the concept that anyone's orientations may change over the course of their life.

(Ace/aro) flux: people who fluctuate along the spectrum, between asexual and allosexual or aromantic and alloromantic. Some people who are aceflux or aroflux will always stay within the asexual or aromantic spectrum, while others may occasionally fall outside of it.

Fray (sexual/romantic): people who only experience attraction to people they are less familiar with. They may lose the attraction entirely upon getting to know the other person. This is sometimes thought of as the opposite of demi(ro).

Gay: a person who experiences attraction or is orientated towards the same gender or people of similar genders. While gay is an orientation label that is commonly used to encompass a variety of attractions, it can be used to refer to any one specific kind of attraction, so someone can identify as gay because they feel same-gender romantic attraction, even if they feel no sexual attraction at all. Gay can also be used as a stand-in label for any queer identity.

Gender binary: the organization of gender into two different, distinct, and opposite types: male/man/masculine and female/woman/feminine. It is created by sociocultural systems and beliefs, and it assumes that masculine and feminine are the "default" or "norm" while anything outside those two categories is wrong or strange.

Gender dysphoria: a feeling of pain, discomfort, disappointment, unhappiness, or "wrongness" that people may experience in relation to their physical body, body image, presentation, or characteristics not matching their sense of gender or internal identity. It is generally felt by transgender and nonbinary people, but not all transgender or nonbinary people feel gender dysphoria, and it is certainly not a prerequisite for the identity.

Gender euphoria: feeling joy, relief, or satisfaction from the realization of a gender identity. This can be inspired just by the discovery of the correct gender identity, performing the correct gender through clothing or accessories, a social transition such as a name or pronoun change, or gender-affirming care.

Gender identity: the personal sense of one's own gender. This can be a conglomeration of one's feelings towards the gender one was assigned at birth, the way that one presents, the dysphoria that one feels, the name and pronouns that one uses, etc.

Gender non-conforming (gnc): when one's gender performance or presentation is considered non-normative for their gender. An androgynous presentation is a form of gender non-conformity, but there are many other ways to be gender non-conforming.

Gender performance or presentation: how one chooses to be perceived as masculine, feminine, androgynous, or nonbinary, and may or may not be connected to one's gender identity. This performance may be shown through clothing, make-up, hairstyle, body art, jewelry, accessories, and attitude.

Genderfluid: a specific nonbinary or genderqueer identity that describes people whose gender identity may shift or who may identify with different genders at different times.

Gray (as in gray-asexual, gray-aromantic, graysexual/gray-sexual, grayromantic/gray-romantic): people who experience attraction only rarely, weakly, under limited circumstances, or in another way that significantly differs from allo(ro)s. This is sometimes used as an umbrella term for people who are aspec but not end-spec aromantic or asexual—in other words, they fall into the gray area between either end of the spectrum—but it is also an orientation label in itself.

Heteronormativity: refers to the assumption, belief, and expectation that people are attracted to people of the "opposite" gender and that this attraction is the "default" or "norm." It is predicated on the gender binary and involves the base assumption that people are cisgender and perisex.

Homophobia: a hatred of, dislike of, fear of, or prejudice against gay people and identities, as well as concepts commonly associated with being gay. Just as being gay is often used as a shorthand for being queer, homophobia is often used as a shorthand for prejudice against queer people and identities.

Intersex: people born with any one of a number of different conditions that lead to various differences in sex characteristics, including chromosomes, genitalia, secondary sex characteristics, and hormones, that do not fit "typical" male or female bodies. Some intersex people may identify as transgender or nonbinary; some may not.

Kink: is often used to refer to BDSM (bondage and discipline, domination and submission, sadism and masochism) and related practices. Kink can include sexual activity or can be non-sexual.

Lesbian: a woman or feminine-aligned person who experiences attraction or is orientated towards the same gender or people of similar genders. While lesbian is an orientation label that is commonly used to encompass a variety of attractions, it can be used to refer to any one specific kind of attraction, so someone can identify as a lesbian because they feel same-gender sexual attraction, same-gender platonic attraction, or same-gender alterous attraction, even if they feel no romantic attraction at all. Lesbians are also not necessarily women.

Lith or akoi (sexual/romantic): two prefixes both used to describe people who may experience attraction and may like the idea of being in a (sexual/romantic) relationship in theory but stop experiencing the attraction if it is reciprocated or if they enter an actual relationship, and they may be uncomfortable with the thought of that happening.

Loveless: a term for aspec individuals, usually aromantic, who do not connect with the word or concept around "love" and prefer to disengage with it altogether.

Lust: experiencing sexual attraction towards someone specific.

Man: someone who identifies as a man. Men usually but not always use he/him pronouns and can have any gender presentation.

Masculine: a set of attitudes, behaviors, or roles commonly associated with men and boys. Note that this is different depending on culture, as there are different associations with men in different cultural contexts, and that being a man is not the same as being masculine. Persons of any gender can take on any and all characteristics of being masculine.

Microlabel: a more specific label under a broader identity label.

Monogamy: the practice of only having one romantic or sexual partner at a time.

Mspec or bi+: shorthand for multi-spectrum, which refers to the host of identities in which people are attracted to or oriented towards multiple genders, including bi, pan, poly, omni, and fluid. This phrase is sometimes used instead of bi+ or bi umbrella so that the bi identity is not privileged above other identities that include attraction to multiple genders.

Nebula (sexual/romantic): people who experience confusion around types of attraction specifically due to their neurodivergence may use the prefix.

Neopronouns: pronouns used, usually by nonbinary or genderqueer people, outside the typical he/she/they/it pronouns. Some examples include fae/faer, xe/xer, bun/buns, and ae/aer. People may use neopronouns if the traditional gendered connotations of pronouns do not feel authentic for them.

Noetic or intellectual attraction: a pull or orientation focused on connecting with someone else's intellect, opinions, or knowledge. It can also focus on the desire to learn from them or become a mentee, or a connection with a mind that functions similarly to one's own.

Nonamorous or nonpartnering: people who do not want any significant or primary partnerships. They may be content being single, living on their own, and getting emotional support from other relationships such as family and friends. They may also have friendships with benefits—friends they have uncommitted sex with—or another form of casual sex in order to fulfill their sexual needs/desires.

Nonbinary (enby or nb) and genderqueer: both umbrella terms for people who do not identify with the gender binary of male and female, as well as identity terms in themselves. These two terms are not interchangeable, because while definitions of each can be subjective, people often attach connotations to each term that change the definition. This means that each individual nonbinary or genderqueer person may have a specific, personal relationship with the definition. Some nonbinary and genderqueer people will identify as trans; some will not.

Omni: people who are attracted to or oriented towards all genders. Unlike pan people, whose attraction is regardless of gender, for omni people, gender does figure into attraction. Unlike most of the other Mspec labels, omni indicates a preference for one or multiple genders (while being attracted to all genders). While omnisexual is an orientation label that is commonly used to encompass a variety of attractions, the omni- prefix may be used to refer to any one specific kind of attraction, such as omniromantic, omnialterous, omnisexual, specifically in reference to sexual attraction, or omniplatonic.

Oriented aroace: an aroace person who is oriented towards a specific gender or genders. In some cases, they are gray (romantic or sexual) and feel oriented when they feel sexual or romantic attraction; in other cases, they feel a specific orientation in a non-romantic or non-sexual attraction.

Otherkin: an umbrella term for those who identify partially or fully as a non-human creature or concept. People who are otherkin recognize that their bodies are human, while their soul, mind, essence, etc. are not. Otherkin identity is not tied to religion, spirituality, or mental health.

Out: when used as an adjective, "out" refers to being known by others to have a certain LGBTQIA+ identity. When used as a verb, "to out someone" refers to someone telling others about someone else's queer identity without their consent.

Pan: people who are attracted to or oriented towards more than one gender, multiple genders, or all genders, or attracted to or oriented towards people regardless of gender. The most common differentiation between pan and bi orientations is that bi people are attracted to multiple genders, though that attraction may be different depending on the gender, while pan people are attracted no matter the gender. However, this distinction is not universal. While pansexual is an orientation label that is commonly used to encompass a variety of attractions, the pan- prefix may be used to refer to any one specific kind of attraction, such as panromantic, panalterous, pansexual, specifically in reference to sexual attraction, or panplatonic.

Perioriented: people whose orientations align. While this can refer to any orientation, based around any kind of attraction, it generally refers to sexual and romantic orientations alone. For example, someone who is demisexual and demiromantic, bisexual and biromantic, or asexual and aromantic.

Perisex or dyadic: people who are not intersex.

Platoni (sexual/romantic): people who cannot distinguish between sexual/romantic and platonic attraction. While similar to quoi, platoni- refers specifically to the confusion around differentiating platonic attraction from other forms of attraction.

Platonic attraction: the desire to form a platonic (non-romantic) relationship with a specific person, usually in the form of a friendship.

Poly: people who are attracted to or oriented towards more than one gender, but not all of them. While polysexual is an orientation label that is commonly used to encompass a variety of attractions, the poly- prefix may be used to refer to any one specific kind of attraction, such as polyromantic, polyalterous, polysexual, specifically in reference to sexual attraction, or polyplatonic.

Polyamory: the practice of consensually having more than one romantic relationship. In some cases, someone will have "primary" and "secondary" relationships; in others, there will be no strict hierarchy.

Pride: in queer or LGBTQIA+ communities, the feeling of happiness or joy in one's queer identity, either displayed publicly (such as through a pride flag) or expressed privately.

Pronoun: the words that are used to refer to someone. They often, but not always, indicate gender.

Queer: an umbrella term for all sexual, romantic, or gender minorities. Can be used as an identity term on its own.

Queerplatonic partnerships/relationships (QPPs or QPRs): relationships that don't fit into the categories of what is traditionally considered to be a friendship or a romantic relationship.

Quoi and wtf (sexual/romantic): prefixes used to describe people who cannot clearly distinguish between different types of attractions or bonds. They may mistake one for the other or not differentiate them at all. These labels also can be used to signify that someone does not find it useful to identify or differentiate attractions.

Recipro (sexual/mantic): people who only experience attraction to a person when/after they know that person is attracted to them. This is sometimes thought of as the opposite of lith(ro).

Relationship anarchy: the ideology and practice of deconstructing amatonormative relationship hierarchies and traditional concepts. Instead of assuming a type of relationship should be a certain way, the dynamic should be discussed and determined by the involved people, and labels should be descriptive of the relationship rather than proscriptive.

Romance-averse: someone who does not want to engage in romantic activities.

Romance-favorable: someone who enjoys or is interested in romantic activities and might want to be in relationships that incorporate them, which they may or may not seek out.

Romance-neutral or romance-indifferent: someone who is neither interested in nor opposed to romantic activities. They may be alright participating in the activities but not seek them out.

Romance-repulsed: finding romantic activity or the idea of romance/romantic activity to be anywhere from uncomfortable, unwanted, or horrific to a traumatic level.

Romantic attraction: an emotional form of attraction that is often separate from other emotional attractions.

Romantic relationship: a relationship between two or more people that includes behaviors that are typically considered "romantic" within the society that the people live in. The specific behaviors that are typically considered "romantic" may differ from society to society and even from relationship to relationship.

Rose: an abbreviation that represents both romantic and sexual, taking the "ro" from "romantic" and "se" from "sexual"—for example, someone who is both demisexual and demiromantic may identify as "demirose" for short.

Sensual attraction: a desire to be physically, non-sexually close to someone specific, through actions such as hugging, cuddling, or holding hands.

Sex-averse: someone who does not want to engage in sexual activities.

Sex-favorable: someone who enjoys or is interested in sexual activities and might want to be in relationships that incorporate them, which they may or may not seek out.

Sex drive or libido: the physical urge for sexual gratification, which can happen even in the absence of a specific person who is found to be attractive.

Sex-negativity or antisexualism: the political or philosophical attitude of being hostile towards certain kinds of or all sexual behavior or sexuality, and the people who engage in it. One expression of sex-negativity is sex shaming or purity culture.

Sex-neutral or sex-indifferent: someone who is neither interested in nor opposed to sexual activities. They may be alright participating in the activities but not seek them out.

Sex-positivity: the political or philosophical attitude supporting people to have as much or as little consensual sexual activity as they want, including consensual sex in all of its varieties. People strongly repulsed by the general idea of sex can still be supportive of others' sexual freedoms.

Sex-repulsed: finding sexual activity or the idea of sex/sexual activity to be anywhere from uncomfortable or unwanted, to horrific or traumatic.

Sexual attraction: the desire for intimate physical or sexual contact with someone. It is a feeling that is directed at specific people.

Sexual desire: wanting to engage in sexual activity; similar to libido, but not necessarily based on a physical urge. Unlike sexual attraction, sexual desire is not directed towards a specific person.

Social dysphoria: when gender dysphoria is experienced around social perceptions and interactions (e.g. being stereotyped based on misgendering) rather than physical appearance.

Soft romo: a low level of romance. For example, this could mean avoiding certain romance-coded activities that trigger a person's romance repulsion or structuring relationship boundaries around an arospec identity (e.g. aroflux).

Split Attraction Model (SAM): one concept of distinguishing between ("splitting") romantic and sexual orientations, and/or other orientations.

Squish: a word to describe the experience of platonic attraction (can be described as a "friend-crush").

Straight: an orientation label for those attracted to a different or dissimilar gender. Straight is sometimes used to mean heteroromantic and heterosexual, but it does not always necessarily refer to being both heteroromantic and heterosexual. Straight used to more commonly reference "opposite gender" attraction, however, it has been changed to reference different and dissimilar gender attraction more broadly, as nonbinary or genderqueer people may be attracted to people of dissimilar genders and gender presentations from their own, and due to being nonbinary or genderqueer, they do not have an opposite gender. Sometimes used, inaccurately, to mean "not queer."

Transgender (trans): people who do not identify as the gender they were assigned at birth. Some trans people will get surgery or hormone therapy to change their physical appearance and body characteristics; some will not.

Two-spirit (also 2S, twospirit, or twospirited): a pan-tribal term originating in 1990 at the Native American/First Nations gay and lesbian conference. It is a culturally closed identity exclusive to North American indigenous people, specifically First Nations/ Native Americans, and can be used to describe someone's gender, sexuality, cultural identity, or spiritual identity. None of them are mutually exclusive to one another, and a two-spirit person may otherwise identify as cisgender and/or heterosexual, or otherwise not queer.

Undirected sex drive: the feeling of arousal that isn't specific to any individual person.

Varioriented: people whose orientations do not align. While this can refer to any orientation, based around any kind of attraction, it generally refers to sexual and romantic orientations alone. For example, someone who is demisexual and aromantic, heterosexual and biromantic, or asexual and allomantic.

Voidpunk: an aesthetic subculture for people who feel dehumanized or rejected by society and reclaim that dehumanization, often by relating to robots, inanimate objects, or aliens.

Woman: someone who identifies as a woman. Women usually but not always use she/her pronouns and can have any gender presentation.

Appendix

This is not a comprehensive list of resources, but will hopefully help guide you to more information about aromanticism and asexuality. We recognize that there are not nearly enough aromantic-specific resources here, in particular resources for allosexual aromantic individuals; unfortunately, that is largely because there are not enough aromantic resources in general. We hope to see many more in the future.

Aromantic and Asexual Organizations

Ace Week

https://aceweek.org

Ace Week is the last full week of October every year and is meant to raise awareness for and celebrate asexuality and bring attention to asexual issues.

Aces and Aros

https://acesandaros.org

This organization exists to empower asexual and aromantic community organizers and activists by providing them with educational resources and tools.

Aromantic Spectrum Awareness Week (ASAW)

www.arospecweek.org

Aromantic Spectrum Awareness Week is the full week after Valentine's Day every year and is meant to raise awareness for and celebrate aromanticism and aromantic people and bring attention to aromantic issues.

Aromantic-spectrum Union for Recognition, Education, and Advocacy (AUREA)

www.aromanticism.org

AUREA is an aromantic-specific organization that advocates for aromantic people's needs and creates resources and community for aros.

Indian Aces

www.indianaces.org

Indian Aces is a large asexuality organization based in India that creates resources and hosts workshops, presentations, and seminars both online and around the world.

International Asexuality Day

https://internationalasexualityday.org/en

A coordinated effort to uplift the work done by ace individuals and organizations around the world, particularly in non-Western and non-anglophone countries, and celebrate them on April 6.

The Ace and Aro Advocacy Project (TAAAP)

https://taaap.org

That's us! We are dedicated to creating and disseminating resources for and about aromantic and asexual people, and to working to create a world that accepts all of our identities.

The Asexuality Visibility and Education Network (AVEN)

www.asexuality.org

AVEN hosts one of the largest communities of asexual people, works towards visibility in media, and hosts conferences.

Aromantic and Asexual Social Groups and Forums

Aces and Aros—Groups

https://acesandaros.org/groups

In addition to online resources, Aces and Aros maintains an extensive list of in-person social groups.

Arocalypse

www.arocalypse.com

Arocalypse is an online forum and community for aromantic people.

Asexual Dating

www.asexuals.net

A dating site specifically for asexual people, as well as a resource of information about asexual and aromantic identities.

TAAAP Pride Chats

https://taaap.org/pride-chat-registration

We host a Discord Server which is open the last weekend of each month as a community space. Each month there is a different main discussion topic, though any participation is welcome.

The Asexuality Visibility and Education Network (AVEN)

www.asexuality.org

AVEN hosts online forums for asexual people.

People to Follow

- Angela Chen (asexual writer)
- Cody Daigle-Orians, Ace Dad (asexual YouTuber and TikToker)
- Elle Rose, or scretladyspider (demisexual activist)
- Marshall Blount, or Gentle Giant Ace (asexual activist and YouTuber)
- Redbeard (asexual and aromantic activist and blogger)
- Sherronda J. Brown (asexual writer)
- Slice of Ace (homoromantic asexual YouTuber)
- swankivy (aromantic asexual YouTuber)
- Yasmin Benoit (aroace activist)

Books (Nonfiction)

Decker, Julie Sondra. *The Invisible Orientation: An Introduction to Asexuality*. Carrel Books, 2014.

The first officially published book on asexuality, this book describes asexuality and how asexuals interact with the world.

Chen, Angela. *Ace: What Asexuality Reveals About Desire, Society, and the Meaning of Sex.* Beacon Press, 2020.

In this book on asexuality, ace writer Angela Chen explores her own identity as she analyzes the impact of compulsory sexuality on our society, particularly on marginalized aces.

Burgess, Rebecca. *How to Be Ace: A Memoir of Growing Up Asexual.* Jessica Kingsley Publishers, 2020.

A graphic novel in which autistic ace artist/writer Rebecca Burgess shares their experience understanding their ace identity as well as their OCD (obsessive-compulsive disorder). It includes "Ace 101" sections interspersed with the narrative.

Brake, Elizabeth. *Minimizing Marriage: Marriage, Morality, and the Law.* Oxford University Press. 2012.

This book discusses the ways that marriage and romance are elevated and prioritized in our society, and how that impacts people who do not want to partner romantically.

DePaulo, Bella. *Singled Out: How Singles Are Stereotyped, Stigmatized, and Ignored, and Still Live Happily Ever After.* St. Martin's Griffin, 2007.

This book destigmatizes singleness and debunks several common myths and stereotypes that are often repeated about the alleged tragedy of being single.

Gahran, Amy. *Stepping Off the Relationship Escalator: Uncommon Love and Life.* Off the Escalator Enterprises LLC, 2017.

Having surveyed over 1500 people for this book, Amy Gahran explains what the traditional expectations are of relationships and then discusses many examples of non-traditional relationships, including ace and aro ones, with real-life examples.

Other Media (Nonfiction)

- *(A)sexual* (2011 documentary film)
- *Asexual: A Love Story* (2016 documentary short film, asexuality)
- *Aromanticism* (2017 studio album) by Moses Sumney
- *Sounds Fake But Okay* (2017–present podcast, one co-host is aromantic asexual, the other is demisexual)
- *The Ace Couple* (2021–present podcast)
- *A-OK* (2019–2020 podcast, asexual and aromantic themed)
- *All Things Aromantic* (2022–present podcast, host is aroace)

Media (Fiction)

The AroAce Database

www.aroacedatabase.com

This is an interactive database with over 600 published works of prose fiction featuring aro or ace characters.

There is no similarly curated list of non-book fiction media, so here is a sampling. (Warning: spoilers for aro or ace characters!)

- *Bloom Into You* (2015–2019 manga and 2018 anime) (Seiji Maki, aromantic asexual)
- *BoJack Horseman* (2014–2020 animated TV series) (Todd, heteroromantic asexual, plus multiple asexual side characters)
- *The Case Files of Jeweler Richard* (2015–present light novel series with manga and anime adaptations) (Shouko Tanimoto, aromantic)

- *Critical Role* (2015–present web series) (Caduceus Clay, aromantic asexual)
- DC's *Legends of Tomorrow* (2016–present live action TV series) (Esperanza "Spooner" Cruz, asexual)
- *Dimension 20: A Crown of Candy* (2020 tabletop role-playing game show) (Liam Wilhelmina, asexual)
- *Emmerdale* (1972–present UK soap opera) (in 2019 introduced Liv Flaherty's asexuality arc)
- *Everything's Gonna Be Okay* (2020–2021 live action TV series) (Drea, homoromantic asexual)
- *The Expanse* (2015–2022 TV series) (Amos Burton, aromantic allosexual)
- *Gargoyles* (1994–1997 animated TV series) (Owen Burnett, asexual)
- *It's Not You, It's Not Me.* (2020 short film, asexuality)
- *Jughead* (2015–2017 comic book) (Jughead, asexual and implied aromantic)
- The Magnus Archives (2016–2021 podcast) (Jonathan Sims, biromantic asexual)
- The Outer Worlds (2019 video game) (Parvati, homoromantic asexual)
- *The Owl House* (2020–present animated TV series) (Lilith Clawthorne, aromantic)
- *Phineas and Ferb* (2007–2015 animated TV series) + *Milo Murphy's Law* (2016–2019 animated TV series) (both take place in the same universe) (Perry the Platypus, asexual)
- *Sex Education* (2019–present live action TV series) (Florence, asexual)
- *Sirens* (2014–2015 live action TV series) (Valentina "Voodoo" Dunacci, asexual)
- *Shadowhunters* (2016–2019 live action TV series) (Raphael Santiago, asexual)
- *Shortland Street* (1992–present New Zealand soap

opera) (in 2007 introduced Gerald Tippett, biromantic asexual)

- *Steven Universe* (2013–2020 animated TV series) (Peridot, ace and aro)

Collections of Aromantic and Asexual Experiences

Ace Zines

https://acezinearchive.wordpress.com

This is a collection of zines available online that focus on asexual experiences.

Aro Zines

https://acezinearchive.wordpress.com/not-specifically-ace -arospec-zines

This is a collection of zines available online that focus on aromantic experiences.

Aspec Voices

https://taaap.org/aspec-voices

These are collections of perspectives from aro and ace people who have specific and distinct experiences in an effort to uplift their voices and show the diversity of these communities.

AZE Journal

https://azejournal.com

AZE Journal is an online publication of agender, aromantic,

and asexual people's creative expressions, including visual art, poetry, essays, and articles.

Carnival of Aces

https://asexualagenda.wordpress.com/a-carnival-of-aces-masterpost

The Carnival of Aces is a community-driven event where a topic is chosen each month and anyone can submit writings about that topic in relation to asexuality. The full submission links for past months are posted to the site above.

Carnival of Aros

https://carnivalofaros.wordpress.com

The Carnival of Aros is a community-driven event where a topic is chosen each month and anyone can submit writings about that topic in relation to aromanticism. The full submission links for past months are posted to the site above.

Aro- and Ace-Specific Resources

Ace Community Survey

https://acecommunitysurvey.org

A community-driven project collecting and analyzing data about the asexual community.

Allosexual Aromantic

https://aroworlds.com/allo-aro

A collection of resources and people to follow for allosexual aromantic people.

Asexual Activities Annex

https://annex.asexualactivities.com

A resource for asexual people to read, learn, and explore more about sexuality from an ace experience.

Asexuality Archive

www.asexualityarchive.com

A repository for resources about asexuality and strategies for ace advocacy.

Asexual Research

https://asexualresearch.omeka.net

A website that collects research on the history of asexuality.

Demisexuality Resource Center

https://demisexuality.org

A collection of information and resources specifically focused on demisexuality.

Disabled Ace Day by Courtney Lane

https://aceweek.org/stories/why-i-m-founding-disabled-ace-day

Courtney Lane, co-host of The Ace Couple podcast and founder of Disabled Ace Day, discusses ableism, aphobia, and the need for more awareness around the challenges that disabled aces face from inside and outside the community. Linked from this article, you can also find articles written by other disabled aces about their experiences.

The Aro Census

www.aromanticism.org/aro-census

A community-driven project collecting and analyzing data about the aromantic community.

The Asexual Agenda Blog

https://asexualagenda.wordpress.com

A blog that collects and disseminates interesting resources on and about asexuality, as well as creating resources itself.

Resources for Ace Survivors

https://asexualsurvivors.org

A project run by ace survivors of sexual violence, the website and associated blogs collect helpful resources specifically for ace survivors of sexual violence. This website also generally provides resources including a printable PDF and links to specific articles that are useful to share with your own health professionals so that they can be better prepared to provide care for asexual patients and clients.

Other Relevant Communities and Resources

10 Principles of Disability Justice, as articulated by Patty Berne and Sins Invalid

www.sinsinvalid.org/blog/10-principles-of-disability-justice

These principles are the essential guideposts for those who fight for disability justice.

Kinmunity Forum

www.kinmunity.com

An online community resource and forum for therian, otherkin, and others with non-human identities.

My Passion Angel

www.mypassionangel.com

Aromantic- and asexual-inclusive sex and relationship education, with a number of resources and exercises specific to aro and ace individuals.

Fun Interactive Resources
Will, Want, Won't List

The Will column is for activities you are comfortable participating in, the Want column is for activities you specifically want to participate in, and the Won't column is for activities you won't participate in, all in a given relationship. While this example list is short and focused on romantic activities, your list can be as long as you want and can be about romantic, sexual, or any other kinds of activities. You can make a list on your own and share it later with the relevant people (friend(s), romantic partner(s), sexual partner(s), etc.), or make the list with them.

This activity was adapted to ace people by Asexual Activities: https://annex.asexualactivities.com/partnered-activities/partnered-general-information/want-will-wont.

EXAMPLE

Will	Want	Won't
Go on dates Dance Give and accept random gifts	Hold hands Cuddling Intimate conversations	Kiss Be called pet names Celebrate Valentine's Day

YOUR TURN!

Will	Want	Won't

Asexual Coming Out Bingo

Asexual Reactions

How can you have a partner then?	It's great that you're saving yourself	I can't imagine being like that	You're just repressed	You're such a nerd/loser
Are you sure you've been doing it right?	You're probably just gay	But you're so attractive!	You are so pure	You're just shy/scared
You've had sex—you can't be asexual	How do you know if you haven't tried it?	**Free** what/huh?	You just haven't met the right person	You must an amoeba/plant
You should get your hormones checked	Isn't that just abstinence/celibacy?	Were you abused?	Wow, you are really immature	You must have a lot of time on your hands
You can get that fixed	You just want to be a snowflake	Do you masturbate?	You just need to have some good orgasms	It's just a phase

Aromantic Coming Out Bingo

Aromantic Reactions

That sounds so lonely!	Did you have a terrible past relationship?	But love makes us human!	Don't give up hope!	I've been thinking I should give up on relation-ships too
It's too hard to keep track of all these new labels	Doesn't that mean you smell nice?	Don't worry, you're still young—you still have time	Sex without romance is so wrong/ disgusting!	Your life must be so simple/easy
But you've been in romances before!	You've never dated anyone— how would you know?	**Free** what/huh?	That's so sad!	You're just scared of commitment
So are you a sociopath/ heartless?	Focusing on your career? Good for you!	How do you cope without a partner?	So you're just a robot	You mean you're asexual right?
But don't you want a big wedding?	So you can't get a date	You haven't met the one yet	What about kids?	That's scientifically impossible /but evolution!

About TAAAP

The Ace and Aro Advocacy Project (TAAAP) is a prominent volunteer-run organization dedicated to providing resources on asexuality and aromanticism to the public. TAAAP is primarily based in the USA, but our advocates reside around the world. All of TAAAP's advocates, including the writers involved in this project, are aromantic and/or asexual.

TAAAP's goals are to increase the visibility of ace and aro identities, to provide resources on asexuality and aromanticism to professionals (e.g. doctors, mental health professionals, educators), and to support ace and aro members of our national and global society. For more information about TAAAP's work or to learn about how you can get involved, visit our website at taaap.org.

Our mission is to:

Tear down the societal norm that romance and sex are required and desired by everyone, and create a society in which all ethical relationship and communal structures are treated equitably.

Advance education and inclusion of aromanticism and asexuality in the public sphere.

Advocate for the recognition and equity of everyone on the ace and aro spectrums, no matter the types of their relationships or lack thereof.

Amplify marginalized voices of the ace and aro communities.

Provide community resources and create community spaces that are by and for aro and ace people first and foremost.

Index

Personal names used as hypothetical examples are given in plain font. Those in italicized font represent quotes. Major mentions are indicated by bold page numbers.

263